THE THIRTY
YEARS' WAR

access to history

in depth

THE THIRTY YEARS' WAR

Graham Darby

Hodder & Stoughton
A MEMBER OF THE HODDER HEADLINE GROUP

Acknowledgements

The front cover illustration shows a portrait of Gustavus Adolphe at the Battle of Breitenfeld by J.J. Walter, reproduced courtesy of Musée Historique de Strasbourg.

The publishers would like to thank the following individuals, institutions and companies for permission to reproduce copyright illustrations in this book: AKG Photo pages 38, 46, 70 and 80.

The publishers would also like to thank the following for permission to reproduce material in this book: Routledge for the extracts from *The Thirty Years' War* by Geoffrey Parker, Routledge, 1984.

Every effort has been made to trace and acknowledge ownership of copyright. The publishers will be glad to make suitable arrangements with any copyright holders whom it has not been possible to contact.

Orders: please contact Bookpoint Ltd, 130 Milton Park, Abingdon, Oxon OX14 4SB. Telephone: (44) 01235 827720, Fax: (44) 01235 400454. Lines are open from 9.00–6.00, Monday to Saturday, with a 24 hour message answering service. Email address: orders@bookpoint.co.uk

British Library Cataloguing in Publication Data
A catalogue record for this title is available from the British Library

ISBN 0 340 780738

First published 2001
Impression number   10 9 8 7 6 5 4 3 2 1
Year   2007 2006 2005 2004 2003 2002 2001

Typeset by Fakenham Photosetting Limited, Fakenham, Norfolk
Printed in Great Britain for Hodder & Stoughton Educational, a division of Hodder Headline Plc, 338 Euston Road, London NW1 3BH by Bath Press Ltd, England.

Contents

Preface

The original *Access to History* series was conceived as a collection of sets of books covering popular chronological periods in British history, together with the histories of other countries, such as France, Germany, Russia and the USA. This arrangement complemented the way in which history has traditionally been taught in sixth forms, colleges and universities. In recent years, however, other ways of dividing up the past have become increasingly popular. In particular, there has been a grater emphasis on studying relatively brief periods in considerable detail and on comparing similar historical phenomena in different countries. These developments have generated a demand for appropriate learning materials, and, in response, two new 'strands' have been added to the main series – *In Depth* and *Themes*. The new volumes build directly on the features that have made *Access to History* so popular.

To the general reader

Access books have been specifically designed to meet the needs of examination students, but they also have much to offer the general reader. The authors are committed to the belief that good history must not only be accurate, up-to-date and scholarly, but also clearly and attractively written. The main body of the text (excluding the Study Guide sections) should therefore form a readable and engaging survey of a topic. Moreover, each author has aimed not merely to provide as clear an explanation as possible of what happened in the past but also to stimulate readers and to challenge them into thinking for themselves about the past and its significance. Thus, although no prior knowledge is expected from the reader, he or she is treated as an intelligent and thinking person throughout. The author tends to share ideas and explore possibilities, instead of delivering so-called 'historical truths' from on high.

To the student reader

It is intended that *Access* books should be used by students studying history at a higher level. Its volumes are all designed to be working texts, which should be reasonably clear on a first reading but which will benefit from re-reading and close study.

To be an effective and successful student, you need to budget your time wisely. Hence you should think carefully about how important the material in a particular book is for you. If you simply need to acquire a general grasp of a topic, the following approach will probably be effective:

1. Read Chapter 1, which should give you an overview of the whole book, and think about its contents.

2. Skim through Chapter 2, paying particular attention to the 'Points to Consider' box and to the 'Key Issue' highlighted at the start of each section. Decide if you need to read the whole chapter.
3. If you do, read the chapter, stopping at the end of every sub-division of the text to make notes.
4. Repeat stage 2 (and stage 3 where appropriate) for the other chapters.

If, however, your course demands a detailed knowledge of the contents of the book, you will need to be correspondingly more thorough. There is no perfect way of studying, and it is particularly worthwhile experimenting with different styles of note-making to find the one that best suits you. Nevertheless the following plan of action is worth trying:

1. Read a whole chapter quickly, preferably at one sitting. Avoid the temptation – which may be very great – to make notes at this stage.
2. Study the diagram at the end of the chapter, ensuring that you understand the general 'shape' of what you have read.
3. Re-read the chapter more slowly, this time taking notes. You may well be amazed at how much more intelligible and straightforward the material seems on a second reading – and your notes will be correspondingly more useful to you when you have to write an essay or revise for an exam. In the long run, reading a chapter twice can, in fact, often save time. Be sure to make your notes in a clear, orderly fashion, and spread them out so that, if necessary, you can later add extra information.
4. The Study Guide sections will be particularly valuable for those taking AS Level, A Level and Higher. Read the advice on essay questions, and do tackle the specimen titles. (Remember that if learning is to be effective, it must be active. No one – alas – has yet devised any substitute for real effort. It is up to you to make up your own mind on the key issues in any topic.)
5. Attempt the source-based question. The guidance on tackling these exercises is well worth reading and thinking about.

When you have finished the main chapters, go through the 'Further Reading' section. Remember that no single book can ever do more than introduce a topic, and it is to be hoped that, time permitting, you will want to read more widely. If *Access* books help you to discover just how diverse and fascinating the human past can be, the series will have succeeded in its aim – and you will experience that enthusiasm for the subject which, along with efficient learning, is the hallmark of the best students.

Robert Pearce

1 Introduction

POINTS TO CONSIDER

This chapter will begin by giving you an outline of the book's contents. It will then go on to introduce you to the historiography of the Thirty Years' War and some of the key questions that have been generated. This will be followed by an introduction to the Holy Roman Empire and the Habsburg family. Your aim should be to keep in mind the key questions, as well as the important events prior to 1618 which form the context for the later years.

KEY DATES

800	Charlemagne establishes the Holy Roman Empire
1356	The Golden Bull designates seven electors to elect the Emperor
1438	All Emperors are chosen from the House of Habsburg from this date
1493	Reign of Maximilian (to 1519): the Imperial Reform Movement
1517	Luther protests: the Reformation begins
1519	Charles V becomes Emperor
1526	Archduke Ferdinand is elected King of Bohemia and Hungary
1555	The Religious Peace of Augsburg
1555/6	Charles V abdicates and divides his territories
1564	Austrian territories sub-divided
1576	Rudolf II becomes Emperor

1 General Outline

> **KEY ISSUE** What are the major issues under discussion in this book?

a) The Origins of the War

Initially this book will look at the general tensions throughout Europe at the beginning of the seventeenth century, in the Baltic, in Italy, between France and Spain, and, in particular, between the Spanish and the Dutch – with the conclusion that perhaps these tensions have more to do with the prolongation of the war than its origins. Then a brief survey of the tensions within Germany will focus on the confessional divide, the crisis over Donauwörth, the rival leagues and the Cleves-Jülich affair with a similar general conclusion that these events too perhaps did not really have anything to do with the outbreak of the war. More crucial by far were the tensions within the Habsburgs' hereditary territories, the *Erbländer*. Accordingly we will focus on the growth of Protestant rights within the Austrian Habsburgs' own territories and the Catholic response under Matthias and Ferdinand. It would appear that it is these events which led to the war. From this perspective the war was in origin an internal Habsburg matter.

b) The Bohemian War 1618–c.1623

However, what began as an internal Habsburg problem soon had wider implications with the involvement of the Spanish, the Catholic League and the Palatinate (among others). The Bohemian rebels were comprehensively defeated but perhaps the Austrian Habsburgs had been too successful for their own good, and now the conflict coalesced with the war between their Spanish cousins and the Dutch. Indeed it was the Dutch who kept the conflict going, first by funding a few German princes and secondly by encouraging Danish intervention.

c) The Danish Episode 1625–29

Although partly funded by the Dutch, Christian IV of Denmark had his own reasons for intervening. However, he too was comprehensively defeated. Once again the Emperor Ferdinand had enjoyed complete success – on this occasion largely due to the generalship of the new Imperial commander, Wallenstein. Now the Emperor was at the peak of his power and in 1629 he issued the Edict of Restitution, a decree designed to recover territory taken from the Roman Catholic church. However, by this stage it was clear that the Habsburgs had been far too successful for their own good. The Emperor had alienated friends as well as enemies – both by the nature of his success and by the arbitrary nature of the Edict. The Imperial Diet at Regensberg in 1630 soon revealed the extent of opposition and indeed the flimsy nature of the Emperor's ascendancy.

d) Swedish Intervention from 1630

At the peak of his power the Emperor had been persuaded to dismiss his controversial general, Wallenstein, but this had left him powerless to repel the Swedish invasion. Gustavus Adolphus, the King of Sweden, intervened in Northern Germany for defensive reasons – he feared a Habsburg invasion; however, later tradition would make out that the salvation of Protestantism was his main motivation. His campaign was astonishingly successful and soon he had reversed the success the Habsburgs had enjoyed over the previous five years. However, his unexpected death in battle in 1632 gave the Emperor an opportunity to recover and Swedish peace feelers were rebuffed. A joint

Austro-Spanish Habsburg army was able to defeat the Swedes at Nördlingen in 1634 and all but won the war. By the Peace of Prague in 1635 both Saxony and Brandenburg agreed terms with the Emperor and for a while it looked as though the war could finally be over. However, at this point the French stepped in to prolong the struggle.

e) French Intervention 1635–48

Cardinal Richelieu, the architect of French foreign policy, was determined to curb Habsburg power and he had for some time been subsidising both Spain and Austria's enemies. In 1635 France went to war with Spain but not Austria. Although the Cardinal agreed to finance Bernard of Saxe-Weimar in his campaigns against the Emperor, it was not until 1638 that France declared war on Austria, after Richelieu had finally reached a favourable deal with the Swedes (a treaty that was renewed in 1641). With the death of Bernard in 1639 the French took control of his army, and these two armies – the Swedes against Imperial forces in Northern Germany and the French against the Catholic League (Bavaria) along the Rhine – gradually wore the Habsburg position down. Whereas previously the war had oscillated back and forth, it was only going one way from the late 1630s and into the 1640s, and not in the Emperor's favour.

By 1642 the tide had clearly turned and serious peace negotiations began in 1643. Of course negotiations were an ongoing process and they proved to be tentative for many years while the campaigning was indecisive. Indeed war itself was indecisive in the early modern period; there were no complete victories, no complete defeats – and this served to prolong the struggle. Sweden's war with Denmark gave the Habsburgs a breathing space but the defeats of 1645 and especially 1648 tipped the scales.

f) The Peace of Westphalia 1648

The terms of the treaty were actually not too bad for the Emperor. Cardinal Mazarin (France's first minister) found that his room for manoeuvre was severely restricted by the outbreak of civil war at home and France did not achieve what it set out to. Nor indeed did the Swedes – so it might appear that the outcome was not a clear-cut matter of victors and vanquished. And although it could be argued that the peace kept Germany divided, equally it could be argued that the longevity of the peace was a measure of its success.

g) The Nature of the War

Finally we will look at some general aspects of the war. The economic and social effects have for long been a matter of historiographical controversy, with some arguing for widespread devastation and others suggesting that exaggeration has distorted the true picture, which for the vast majority was really not so bad. More recently a measure of consensus has been achieved and the feeling now is that while some areas were indeed devastated others were not. What is clear is that while some areas were subject to constant campaigning others were completely untouched.

Equally controversial is the religious nature of the war. Was this the last religious war, as many books suggest? If it was, what do we make of the campaigns against the Turks in the 1680s? Did it begin as a religious war and end up a political one? And was the war part of a 'Military Revolution'? All these issues will be addressed.

2 The Key Questions

> **KEY ISSUES** Was the Thirty Years' War a) only part of a general, longer war or b) a single war in its own right or c) made up of several separate, distinct conflicts?

Was there ever a Thirty Years' War? This may seem to be a strange way to begin a book with that title, but for many years it was quite fashionable to question its very existence. In particular the historians Saul Steinberg, T.K. Rabb and Henry Kamen all expressed reservations.[1]

The concept of a single war could be criticised from two seemingly contradictory perspectives. On the one hand, the Thirty Years' War could be seen as consisting of a series of separate, distinct conflicts with little connection or coherence; on the other hand, it could be viewed as only part of a much larger, longer, broader European struggle. These two formulations could in fact be reconciled by identifying just some of the episodes as part of the broader conflict and seeing others as separate and different.

Thus the early phase, the Bohemian War (1618–1623), could be seen simply as a revolt within the Habsburg hereditary territories. The subsequent Danish and Swedish phases (c. 1625–1635) could be seen as part of the struggle for the domination of the Baltic: and the final or French phase (1635–1648) could be seen as part of the general struggle for hegemony in Europe (which did not achieve resolution until 1659).

Even those historians who entitled their works 'The Thirty Years' War' often brought different perspectives to the same events. Thus while C.V. Wedgwood (1938) saw the war as essentially a German conflict (a not unreasonable positon to take), the French historian Georges Pagés (1939) was obsessed by the importance of the role of France (and it was an important role). J.V. Polisensky (1971), on the other hand, saw his native Bohemia as central to the whole conflict, a position more difficult to sustain. Saul Steinberg (1966) saw the main issue as the contest between France and Spain, which according to him began in 1609 (despite the fact that the really decisive clash did not begin until 1635) and lasted until 1659.[2] Still more recently in 1992 Nicola Sutherland contended that the war was part of a Franco-Spanish struggle that went back to the 1490s and was not resolved until 1743! She describes the Thirty Years' War as 'a largely factitious conception which has, nevertheless, become an indestructable myth'.[3] Of course (leaving aside the use of the word 'myth') it might be indestructible because it might just reflect what actually happened!

The truth is that because of its complexity the Thirty Years War is a particularly difficult subject to grasp: it is very easy to be confused by the different participants, their different motives and their limited intervention. It is often hard to see any common theme – or if it had a common theme it might not be seen as common to all these thirty years. For these reasons the war can easily dissolve into a series of separate wars, or become immersed in a broader conflict, as many of these historians have contended.

Any revisionist challenge to historical orthodoxy can be a healthy process: it can force historians to look afresh at the familiar with a more critical eye. It can take us one step closer to the truth, by uncovering new evidence or by taking a new perspective or by achieving greater objectivity. However, sometimes historians challenge an orthodoxy for its own sake and their challenge possesses little of substance beyond the challenge itself and rarely if ever offers any satisfactory alternative.

There is no doubt that the war can be looked at in a variety of different ways and it was at times both disjointed and composite; but the term 'the Thirty Years' War' has a practical use – that is to say, it is a label that does seem to reflect the events it describes. Apart from the fact that it is more difficult to identify coherence over an even longer period (as Steinberg and Sutherland have unsuccessfully attempted to do), the problem with this attack on the concept of the Thirty Years' War is that it completely ignores those aspects of the war that do give it coherence (of which more later) and it also completely ignores the way contemporaries viewed the events. The war was seen by them as a continuous conflict that lasted for thirty years. Indeed contemporaries spoke of a fifteen years' war in 1633, a twenty years' war in 1638 and so on. In May 1648, even before the fighting stopped, one of the delegates at the peace negotiations is on record as referring to 'the thirty years' war' that had ravaged his country. And not long after the Peace of Westphalia brought war to an end in October 1648 a pamphlet entitled, 'A Short Chronicle of the Thirty Years' War' provided German readers with information about many of the events of the recent war. In February 1649 the English weekly paper *The Moderate Intelligencer* began to publish a series of articles entitled 'An Epitome of the late Thirty Years' War in Germany', starting with the Bohemian War, 1618–23 followed by the Dutch and Danish phases and so on.[4]

These of course were views from a Protestant perspective and Catholic observers saw the events a little differently, though for them opposition to the Emperors Ferdinand II and Ferdinand III was the common theme. Many distinguished between the internal opposition of the 1620s (i.e. in Bohemia) and that of foreign opposition after 1630 (from Sweden and France). And yet still the title stuck and went largely unchallenged for 300 years.

Now we have to ask ourselves why contemporaries did adopt this label – it must be because they believed it to be true. After all we should remember that many labels – the Counter Reformation, the Dutch Revolt, the Age of Absolutism etc. – are historians' inventions and would not be recognised by contemporaries. That the Thirty Years' War would be, perhaps gives this label a certain pedigree. And in any event it was adopted with good reason. The war had a geographical coherence – it was fought out in the Holy Roman Empire, in Germany. It was a 'German War', as one contemporary put it. It had a political coherence – it was fought out to determine Austrian Habsburg political power within the Holy Roman Empire. These are factors that gave the war a coherence, a beginning and an end. Of course the war was episodic but the Austrian Habsburgs, the Holy Roman Empire and Germany seem to be common to all the episodes. It would be tempting also to suggest that the war had a religious coherence – Catholic versus Protestant – but that would not be strictly true, important though that conflict was at the beginning, through the 1620s, at the peace table and to many contemporaries throughout (see page 90).

Of course you may decide that this matter is unresolved and that it is still a valid question to consider whether or not there was such a thing as the Thirty Years' War. This question is in fact only one of many thrown up by all this historical debate. Others which will have to be addressed during the course of this book include:

- Was it one war or many?
- Was it only part of a wider European struggle?
- Why did the war break out when it did?
- Why did it last so long?
- What was the impact of foreign intervention?
- What was at stake?
- Was it a religious war?
- What were the economic and social effects?
- What was the outcome?
- Was it a defeat for the Habsburgs?
- Did the French achieve their aims?
- Did the war retard German development?

3 The Holy Roman Empire

> **KEY ISSUE** What was the Holy Roman Empire?

a) Origins

The western half of the Roman Empire officially came to an end in AD 476 with the deposition of the last Emperor, Romulus Augustulus. For reasons that are not entirely clear Charlemagne, the ruler of the Franks, reconstituted the *Imperium Romanum* in the year AD 800 with his coronation as Holy Roman Emperor in Rome. However, the empire in this form, covering what is today much of France, Italy and Germany, did not last long and it soon split into three regions. The eastern region, which was known as 'Germany' after its predominant language, retained the title 'Holy Roman Empire', despite the fact that *Germania* had never been part of the Roman Empire. This area evolved as a region of overlapping feudal jurisdictions (i.e. a number of small separate states), a tendency which continued under the three great dynasties of the late medieval period (Ottonian, Salian, and Staufer). Indeed from 1273 the practice of electing each new emperor (just as the Pope is elected by the princes of the church, the cardinals) further weakened the position of the monarchy by preventing any continuity. By the Golden Bull of 1356 the seven leading princes of the Empire were designated the sole electors – that is to say, the Archbishops of Mainz, Cologne and Trier, and the rulers of Brandenburg, Saxony, Bohemia and the Palatinate. In this way then the Emperor became little more than a figurehead with little real power over a myriad of different jurisdictions. It was a prestigious title, but little else. However, this system only brought disorder to Germany, and from 1438 – in an effort to create political stability and continuity – the electors chose their Emperors from a single family, the House of Habsburg, though there developed a tension between the Habsburg emperor's private, dynastic interest and his wider imperial interests.

b) Geography

By the late fifteenth century the empire had become known as the Holy Roman Empire of the German Nation, a title that was formally adopted in 1512. However, at no time did the Empire encompass a single linguistic or national group. Although by this period the core area consisted of what is today Germany and Austria, it also encompassed Luxemburg, Belgium, Holland, part of Burgundy (then called Franche Comté) and the Czech and Slovak Republics (then known as the kingdom of Bohemia with its dependencies, Moravia, Lusatia and Silesia); in addition, Switzerland and some principalities and cities of northern Italy were formally part of the Empire but were in practice only very loosely associated with it. Within 'Germany', the core, there were over 1,000 separate political units, many very small, including 400 or so Imperial Knights who might each own only part of a village. On the other hand some jurisdictions were quite large: leaving aside Habsburg territory, the largest states were Saxony, Brandenburg and Bavaria, followed by the Palatinate, Hesse, Trier and Württemberg – though the Palatinate was divided and Hesse too came to be divided.

Thus the Empire was vast, cosmopolitan and diverse. The Emperor's authority over it was far from uniform and he only ruled directly in his own personal, dynastic possessions. The electors, along with other princes, feudal lords, clerics, ecclesiastical institutions, autonomous cities and village communes held the rest of the land through a complex system of ownership. Indeed it was this fragmented sovereignty and diffusion of political power that has given the Holy Roman Empire such a bad press. German scholars in the nineteenth century regarded decentralised political power as a weakness which had held up national unification (Germany was not unified until 1871) and relegated 'Germany' to a peripheral historical role for centuries. Accordingly the view took hold that because the Empire had failed to become a modern state, it had been rendered incapable of stemming the tide of the Reformation and incapable of preventing the devastation of the Thirty Years' War. In short, the Holy Roman Empire was a disaster, a shambles, a failure, and after 1648 forever in a state of decline and near collapse. However, more recently historians have learnt to take a different approach (an example of revisionism that has borne fruit) and have come to view the Empire on its own terms. Seen in this light the Empire and its institutions take on a positive light and are seen as vibrant and useful. The Empire served a purpose, was valued by its members and its institutions evolved and adapted to changing circumstances.

c) Organisation

How was the Empire organised? It had a peculiar 'mulitilayered political structure subordinate to the Emperor's overall authority, but not his direct control.'[5] However, by the late 15th century the exact nature of power and responsibility within the Empire was far from clear. Disillusion with Frederick III (1440–1493) led to what has become known as the 'imperial reform' movement. Because his successor Maximilian I (1493–1519) was preoccupied with dynastic considerations he was prepared to make changes. Thus from 1495 the *Reichstag*, the main assembly, became the forum for debate; in 1495 and 1498 the two imperial courts, the *Reichskammergericht* and the *Reichshofrat*, were established; and subsequently the Empire was subdivided into regions known as *Kreise* or Circles.

Most electors feared Imperial Absolutism (that is to say, they feared

The Holy Roman Empire *c.* 1618

the Emperor extending his direct control over the empire itself), but there is little evidence that any Emperors ever seriously thought of doing this: their pretensions were dynastic rather than imperial. Yet to forestall any moves towards more direct imperial rule, the territorial rulers tended to champion their right of representation at the national level. In this way they contributed to the development of institutions like the *Reichstag* and the Circles. In any event, the sheer extent of the Empire exceeded the contemporary capacity for centralised administration; key functions had to be devolved to the territories and the Circles. Although the emergence of distinct territories within the Empire was a major long-term trend, only a few of them possessed the potential to survive as viable independent states outside the imperial structure. Hence most wanted an active Emperor who would advance the wider common interest. There was concern over weak or unstable Emperors such as Rudolf II (1576–1612) and Matthias (1612–1619), just as there was concern with Emperors perceived to be too preoccupied with dynastic interests, like Frederick III, Maximilian and, of course, Charles V (1519–1556).

i) The Emperor's Powers
What were the Emperor's powers? He had important feudal powers and could dispense patronage, by creating noble titles, making church appointments, appointing judges to the Imperial Courts and by setting the agenda for the Reichstag. However, from 1519 he needed the Electors' approval to declare war and he came to share power with the Reichstag over legislation and in fiscal (money), military and diplomatic matters – though he could raise taxes for defence, against the Turkish threat in particular. However, tax raising actually strengthened the princes as they were made responsible for its collection and this legitimised their own embryonic fiscal systems. Imperial rule gradually lost its feudal character as time passed and the Emperor's position as the defender of the Catholic Church was undermined by the Reformation.

The Emperors

Frederick III	1440–1493
Maximilian I	1493–1519
Charles V	1519–1556
Ferdinand I	1556–1564
Maximilian II	1564–1576
Rudolf II	1576–1612
Matthias	1612–1619
Ferdinand II	1619–1637
Ferdinand III	1637–1657

ii) The Reichstag
The *Reichstag* originated in the electoral meetings held during *inter-*

regna (i.e. between the death of one Emperor and the election of another) but it became a much larger body. It was not representative – it was an assembly of privileged princes, both secular and ecclesiastical (such as Archbishops) and later included counts and prelates (for instance, bishops), and imperial or free cities (i.e. those cities that had developed outside the boundaries of imperial and territorial fiefs). In its final form it consisted of three *curia* or assemblies. The first was the assembly of (seven) electors which had been established in 1273; the second was the assembly of princes both secular and ecclesiastical, which had emerged by 1480 – numbers here grew in the 16th century from about 100 to between 200–300. The assembly of the imperial cities (never more than 87) evolved from civic conferences of the 15th century and were allowed to participate in the *Reichstag* from 1582; however, they were not formally confirmed as a third assembly until 1648.

Meetings almost always took place in Regensburg or Augsburg and sessions (there were 40–45 between 1495 and 1654) lasted between five weeks and ten months. Despite acute religious polarisation in the years 1576 to 1603, the *Reichstag* continued to function, held together by fear of the Turkish threat. But soon after it did become deadlocked.

iii) The Imperial Courts

The Imperial Courts were established to replace personalised justice (i.e. justice dispensed solely by the Emperor) by an autonomous court of appeal which would be unbiased. The *Reichskammergericht* (Imperial Chamber Court) was established in Speyer in 1495 and Maximilian established the rival *Reichshofrat* (Aulic Council) in Prague (later Vienna) in 1498 (Burgundy, Holland, Belgium, Luxemburg and Franche Comté were exempt). The Supreme Courts were slow and conservative but tended to reach workable, compromise decisions, and they proved to be a useful substitute for violence. However, by the end of the sixteenth century religious differences led to their breakdown, as increasingly decisions were felt to be biased and were therefore ignored.

iv) The Circles

Of greater significance perhaps were the *Kreise* or Circles established to devolve responsibiltiy for defence and maintain public order. Six were established in 1500 and four more in 1512. Again Burgundy was excluded (later by virtue of its transfer to the Spanish branch of the Habsburg family in 1548) as were the kingdom of Bohemia and its associated principalities.

The Circles were not just concerned with military matters and public order but came to be involved in fiscal management and the selection of judges to the *Reichskammergericht*. The *Kreis* structure also provided the infrastructure small states were unable to develop for themselves, and because of this the most active Circles were those which contained a greater proportion of weaker territories. Other Circles came to be dominated by the larger territories (e.g. Bavaria, Saxony etc).

v) The Imperial Church

The Imperial Church consisted of a large number of ecclesiastical territories (the 1521 tax list contained 50 ecclesiastical princes and 83 prelates) and three of the seven electors were churchmen. The Imperial Church enjoyed a close relationship with the Emperor who was the defender of Catholicism. However, as we have indicated, the emergence of Protestantism after 1517 created a permanent confessional divide.

For one thing, it led to the secularisation of church lands – that is to say, Catholic Church land was taken over by Protestants. This was done either by the personal conversion of a bishop or archbishop, who would then turn his land into a secular principality, or, more commonly, by the annexation and incorporation of the land by neighbouring secular Protestant territories when ecclesiastical foundations and sees fell vacant. Württemberg, Hessen and Saxony all expanded their lands considerably by this method. The Religious Peace of Augsburg of 1555 was designed to halt his process (see the box on the Peace).

In addition, confessional strife both contributed to and served as an excuse for political rivalries between the princes. The Protestant princes formed the Schmalkaldic League in 1531. Defeat of the League in 1547 gave Charles V the opportunity to impose a settlement in the 'Interim' of 1548 but it proved unstable. The Religious Peace of Augsburg was largely the work of Charles's brother Ferdinand and represented a prime example of consensus politics in the Empire. The Peace was flawed but recent research has focused on why it lasted so long rather than on why it failed. After all the Holy Roman Empire avoided war in the 16th century unlike neighbouring France, which slipped into a violent religious civil war. Both Ferdinand I (1556–1564) and Maximilian II (1564–1576) were clearly committed to making it work.

However, fail it did. It proved impossible to enforce, and secularisation continued apace throughout the 1560s, 1570s and 1580s. This dramatically reduced the size of the Imperial Church inclining it towards greater dependency on the Emperor. Gradually the competing churches defined their differences ever more precisely: division became permanent; and of course secularisation reinforced territorialisation. However, the progressive disintegration of the settlement after 1576 owed much to Habsburg disunity and the complex personality of the Emperor Rudolf II (1516–1612). To the Habsburgs we now turn.

THE RELIGIOUS PEACE OF AUGSBURG 1555

The Peace of Augsburg recognised the right of each secular territorial ruler to dictate whether his subjects' religion was to be Catholic or Lutheran (Calvinism was not included – in fairness it had not made much impact on Germany at this stage). Later this principle became known as *cuius regio, eius religio* (literally 'whose territory, his religion'). The only exceptions were the Imperial Free Cities and the Catholic ecclesiastical states. In the eight cities which at the time were neither entirely Catholic nor entirely Lutheran, both faiths were, in theory, to coexist in parity. As far as Catholic ecclesiastical states were concerned, if a bishop or archbishop became a Lutheran, he was to resign so that a Catholic could be elected in his place, thus ensuring that the territory would remain Catholic. The Archbishop of Cologne who converted to Protestantism was forced to do this by Spanish and Bavarian troops in the 1580s. This measure, the Ecclesiastical Reservation (*reservatum ecclesiasticum*), was included in the Peace without Protestant consent as an Imperial decree, not by the vote of the Diet. Finally there was a secret assurance (the *Declaratio Ferdinandi*) that nobles and towns already Lutheran within Catholic ecclesiastical territories prior to 1555 could continue to exercise their religion; however, this was not binding in law. Indeed much was unclear and both sides appealed to the Imperial courts for clarification, though Protestants came to distrust the decisions as Catholic judges were in the majority. Another complication was the rapid growth of Calvinism after 1555, a denomination not recognised by the Peace.

4 The Habsburgs

KEY ISSUE How did the Habsburgs rise to power and where did they rule?

The rise of the Habsburg family is a remarkable one, largely the result of dynastic marriage and fortuitous inheritance. Historical scholarship has not succeeded in making the family's origins completely clear; however, the name is derived from the castle of Habichtsburg built in 1020 in what is now Switzerland. Werner I (died 1096) bore the title count of Habsburg but the age-long identification of the Habsburgs with Austria begins in 1273 when Rudolf I was elected king of Germany and later in 1282 when he bestowed Austria and Styria on his two sons. The continuous line of Habsburg Emperors began in 1438 with Albrecht II. The hereditary lands of the Habsburgs by this stage formed an aggregate large enough and rich enough to make

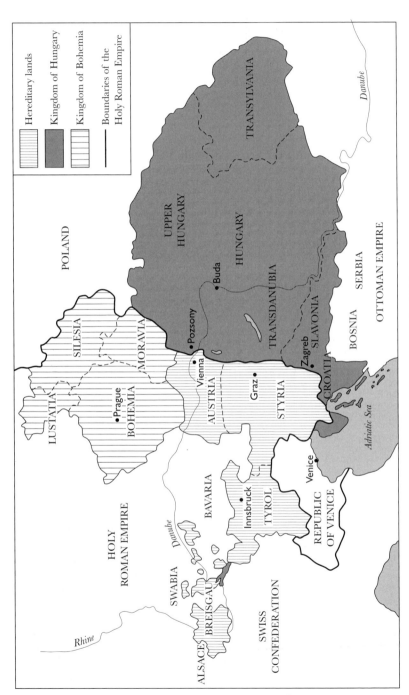

The Austrian Monarchy 1526

Legend:
- Hereditary lands
- Kingdom of Hungary
- Kingdom of Bohemia
- Boundaries of the Holy Roman Empire

POLAND

TRANSYLVANIA

Danube

UPPER HUNGARY

HUNGARY

SERBIA

OTTOMAN EMPIRE

SILESIA

MORAVIA

Buda

TRANSDANUBIA

LUSATIA

Pozsony

Vienna

BOSNIA

Prague

BOHEMIA

AUSTRIA

Graz

STYRIA

Zagreb

SLAVONIA

CROATIA

Adriatic Sea

HOLY ROMAN EMPIRE

BAVARIA

Innsbruck

TYROL

Venice

REPUBLIC OF VENICE

SWABIA

Danube

BREISGAU

ALSACE

SWISS CONFEDERATION

Rhine

the dynasty one of the foremost families in the Empire and therefore the obvious choice for the imperial title. The hereditary territories, or *erbländer* as they were known, consisted of Austria, Carinthia, Styria, Carniola, the Tyrol, Alsace, Breisgau and some lands adjacent to the Danube, as can be seen on the map on page 14.

In 1477 Frederick III's son Maximilian married Mary of Burgundy and their son Philip inherited much of the Burgundian inheritance including what is today Holland, Belgium and Luxembourg as well as Franche-Comté (the 'free county' of Burgundy as opposed to the duchy which was in France). In 1496 Maximilian procured Philip's marriage to Joan the heiress of Castile (and future conquests in America) and Aragon (which included the Balearics, Sardinia, Naples and Sicily). Philip was briefly King of Castile but died prematurely; however, all this territory came to reside in a single person, the Emperor Charles V (1519–1556), who added the duchy of Milan. However, this proved too much for one man to govern and as early as 1522 he assigned the hereditary territories in the Empire to his brother Ferdinand, who himself was elected King of Bohemia and Hungary in 1526 to meet the Turkish threat (to make sense of this it is essential you look at the family tree on page 16).

It was also agreed that Ferdinand should follow Charles as Emperor and he was elected King of the Romans in 1531. However, as Charles wished to leave the bulk of his territory to his son, Philip, he became reconciled to the division of the dynasty. In Brussels between October 1555 and January 1556 Charles V abdicated all his imperial, royal and princely titles, leaving the lion's share to his son Philip II of Spain (i.e. Burgundy/the Netherlands, Spain, the Americas and the Italian possessions). Although Ferdinand became Emperor, the 'Spanish' presence in northern Italy and Burgundy (or the Netherlands as it is better known) largely removed these areas from imperial jurisdiction. Northern Italy had for some considerable time been peripheral and in 1548 Charles had made special arrangements to make the 17 provinces of the Netherlands a single Habsburg hereditary state. Thus it was that the two branches of the family, Spanish and Austrian, came into being.

Although the Austrian branch was the poorer relation it did not become really weak until after 1564. In that year Ferdinand I died and divided his territories up between his three sons: the duchies of Styria, Carinthia, and Carniola with their capital at Graz were left to the youngest, Charles; the Tyrol ruled from Innsbruck went to the middle son Ferdinand; and Austria, together with Bohemia and Hungary, was left to the eldest son, who also became Emperor Maximilian II (see the map on page 17).

Habsburg authority within the hereditary territories was further diluted by the growth of representative assemblies in all the Austrian duchies, largely dominated by the aristocracy, after 1564; and by the growth of Protestantism. By 1580 it has been estimated that some

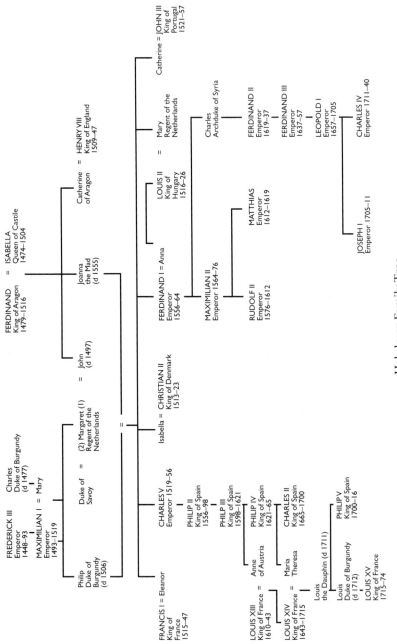

Habsburg Family Tree

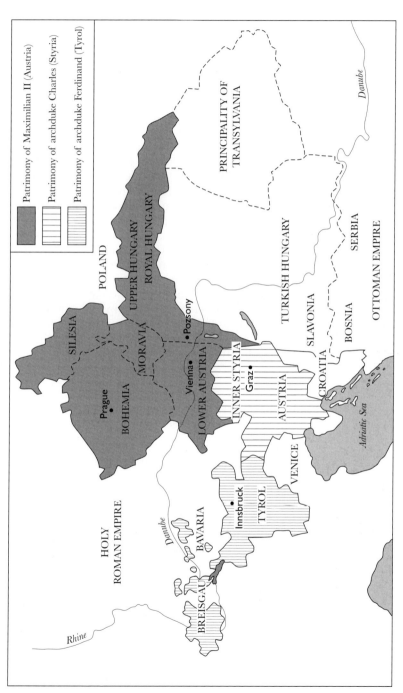

The division of 1564

90 per cent of the nobles in Austria were Protestant. Moreover in 1568 and 1571, in return for taxes for defence against the Turks, Maximilian II granted freedom of worship to Lower Austria. In 1578 the Protestant-led Estates of Upper Austria secured similiar concessions from the new Emperor Rudolf II, and Archduke Charles was also forced to do the same in the duchies of Carinthia, Carniola and Styria. However, this was a situation that could not be allowed to continue – it was the ruler not the ruled who was supposed to determine a state's religion. From the 1590s the Habsburgs hit back. Ferdinand II of Styria, the new Archduke, proved particularly effective in eliminating Protestantism in his duchies. However, Rudolf II's attempts to eliminate Protestantism in Hungary were quite pointless given that there were hardly any Catholics left in that kingdom. Indeed the collapse of Habsburg authority and the gradual breakdown of imperial institutions owed a great deal to the complex personality of Rudolf II. He showed more interest in erotica and alchemy than government and spent long periods in self-imposed isolation in his palace in Prague. By 1598 he was leaving many documents unsigned, paralysing imperial and Habsburg administration and creating a dangerous power vacuum in both the Empire and the hereditary lands. As the seventeenth century dawned the religious split, imperial paralysis and Habsburg weakness all constituted a potentially volatile cocktail. Of course this situation did not make war inevitable but it did require some resolution – and is the subject of the next chapter.

References

1   T.K. Rabb (ed.), *The Thirty Years' War* (Lexington, 1964) and his 'The effects of the Thirty Years' War on the German economy', *Journal of Modern History*, 34 (1962), pp. 40–51; S.H. Steinberg, 'The Thirty Years' War: a new interpretation', *History* (1947), pp. 89–102; and H. Kamen, 'The economic and social consequences of the Thirty Years' War', *Past and Present*, 39 (1968), pp. 44–61.

2   S.H. Steinberg, *The Thirty Years' War and the Conflict for European Hegemony* (New York, 1966).

3   N.M. Sutherland, 'The origins of the Thirty Years' War and the structure of European politics', *English Historical Review*, 107 (1992), p. 587.

4   See Ronald G. Asch, *The Thirty Years' War* (Macmillan, 1997), p. 3 and Geoffrey Parker (ed.), *The Thirty Years' War* (Routledge, 1984), p. xiii.

5   Peter H. Wilson, *The Holy Roman Empire 1495–1806* (Macmillan, 1999), p. 9.

Summary Diagram
The Phases of the War

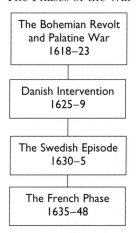

The Bohemian Revolt
and Palatine War
1618–23

Danish Intervention
1625–9

The Swedish Episode
1630–5

The French Phase
1635–48

Working on Chapter 1

Note-making is the foundation of all your learning – the basis for both essay writing and revision. It is also an active process that requires you to concentrate while you read. The subdivisions of this chapter make it relatively easy to decide on headings, but deciding on the level of content is not so easy. Do not write out the whole book – there is no point – but on the other hand make sure you do not miss anything important. This is not an easy task when you are unfamiliar with a topic.

This chapter is essentially introductory; but it is important you absorb the background material. It is divided into four sections.

i) The first section deals with the historiography of the subject and identifies a number of key questions raised by historians' investigations. It is essential you keep these questions in mind as you read through the book.

ii) The second section is an overview of the book and is subdivided a) to g), roughly corresponding to the chapters in the book.
The next two sections deal with the background to the seventeenth century by looking at:

iii) The Holy Roman Empire – this section is divided up by the headings:
Origins
Geography
Organisation

iv) The Habsburg Family – this is largely a chronological history.
This background material should give you some idea of the complex political geography of both the Empire and the Habsburg hereditary territories within it – as well as some appreciation of the religious and political problems that needed some sort of resolution.

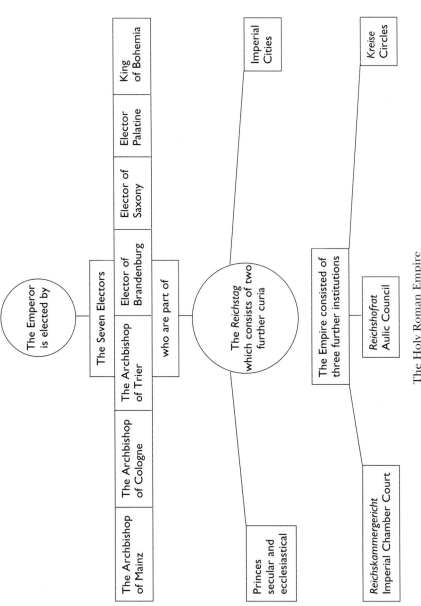

The Holy Roman Empire

2 The Causes of The Thirty Years' War

POINTS TO CONSIDER

This chapter will look at the sources of tension across Europe, inside the Holy Roman Empire, and within the Habsburgs' hereditary territories. You have to decide what contribution each of these made to the outbreak of the war in 1618.

KEY DATES

1600		Sigismund, King of Sweden and Poland is deposed in Sweden
1606		Toleration granted in Hungary; Peace with Turkey
1607		Donauwörth incident
1608	**May**	Formation of the Evangelical Union
	June	Deposition of Rudolf as King of Hungary – Matthias elected in his place
1609		Cleves-Jülich Affair begins
	March	Matthias grants toleration in Austria
	April	Twelve Year Truce between Spain and the Dutch is signed
		Emperor Rudolf grants Letter of Majesty in Bohemia
	July	Formation of Catholic League
1610		Henry IV of France assassinated
1611		Rudolf replaced as King of Bohemia by Matthias
1612		Rudolf dies; Matthias becomes Emperor
1613		Peace between Sweden and Denmark
1614		Closure of Protestant church at Klostergrab
1617		Ferdinand of Styria made King-designate in Bohemia
1618	**May**	Defenestration of Prague – Bohemian revolt begins
	Aug	Fall of Oldenbarnevelt
	Oct	Fall of Lerma

Students can be forgiven for getting muddled when trying to identify the causes of the Thirty Years' War. Many of the books on the subject confound the reader with complex discussions about general long-term political and religious tensions throughout Europe and within the Holy Roman Empire. But the Thirty Years' War did not begin as a result of these general tensions; it began as an internal Habsburg dispute, a rebellion against Habsburg government and religious policy in Bohemia. That this soon developed Europe-wide implications and coalesced with other long-term factors was the result of the rebellion and the way it unfolded, rather than its cause.

So why have so many books concentrated on other issues, such as Baltic tensions and Spanish rivalry with the Dutch and the French?

Well, there is no doubt that these factors are important for the war, but as we have indicated, only as reasons for its development and prolongation. If we look at them in a little detail we can see that this is the case. And what of those famous German crises, the Donauwörth incident and the Cleves-Jülich affair, usually held up as examples of the inevitability of religious conflict? What is actually most striking about them is the fact that they did *not* lead to war. Indeed the majority of German rulers were far more afraid of war than desired it.

KEY ISSUE What were the areas of potential conflict in Europe?

---

1 Tensions in Europe

Rivalry in the Baltic between Sweden and Denmark was of long standing. Sweden had broken away from Denmark in the early sixteenth century and it was an objective of Danish policy to recover Swedish territory. The rivalry between Sweden and Poland, by contrast, was more recent and dated from the time when Sigismund Vasa was both King of Poland (from 1587) and Sweden (from 1592). As he was a Catholic, he was deposed in Sweden in 1600 by his uncle who became Charles IX in 1604. Thus there was dynastic and religious rivalry between two branches of the same family, the legitimist Catholic line in Warsaw and the Protestant usurpers in Stockholm. These two rivalries did have an impact on the war once it was under way, particularly in the 1620s and 1640s, but not in the period up to 1618. Sweden and Denmark made peace in 1613 and a truce was signed between Sweden and Poland in 1618. The Baltic was at peace when the Thirty Years' War broke out.

Clearly the Dutch had an interest in what was going on in the Baltic since their merchants controlled the bulk of the trade in that area. However, of greater significance was their struggle with Spain, since the Dutch had been locked in a war for independence for several decades. There is no doubt that this conflict was to exercise a decisive impact on the war after the Bohemian rebellion, but prior to it the two countries were at peace, having signed a Twelve Year Truce in 1609, and they were at pains to maintain it. Indeed Lerma, Philip III's first minister, and Oldenbarnevelt, the effective ruler of the Dutch Republic, worked hard to bring about a full peace, but it was not to be. Moreover, subsequent internal religious and political squabbles ensured that the Dutch were in no position to intervene in 1618 when the war broke out.

In order to sustain its war with the Dutch the Spanish had developed a military supply route – the Spanish Road – from Italy to Flanders. However, what was a lifeline to Spain was a noose to France, and the location of Spanish territory to the north, the Spanish Netherlands (Flanders and Luxemburg), to the east in Franche Comté, and to the south, in Rousillon and the Pyrenees – not to mention Spanish territory in Italy (Milan, Naples and Sicily) – made the French feel encircled. It was a primary aim of French policy to break this encirclement. However, during the second half of the sixteenth century France had been plunged into civil war – the French Wars of Religion – and it was only with the accession of Henry IV (in 1589) that French foreign policy developed some coherence. In 1601 Henry had forced Savoy to cede territory to the west of the Rhone which had threatened the Spanish Road and in 1610 it had seemed likely that some confrontation would occur over the Cleves-Jülich affair. However, at that point Henry IV was assassinated and the Duke of Lerma was able to take advantage of Queen Marie de Medici's goodwill and effect a full rapprochement, culminating in a double marriage (in 1615). Although Marie's rule ended in 1617 and Lerma fell from power in 1618, there was to be no significant direct confrontation between these two powers for some time. Until Richelieu finally sorted out the internal Huguenot (Protestant) problem in 1629 (which in effect ended the Wars of Religion) and defeated the pro-Spanish *dévot* party (see glossary) in 1630, France would play a minor role in the war. It is true that thereafter her role would become increasingly decisive, but that was a long way off in 1618.

The vast territories of the Spanish Habsburg Monarchy were difficult to govern and difficult to defend. Spanish policy, though often interpreted as aggressive, was in fact usually defensive, concerned as it was with simply maintaining its hold over its possessions and protecting communications between them. Madrid's principal concern was to effect a reasonable settlement with the Dutch, one that would not be bad for Spain's reputation. A defeat, it was felt, would have a domino effect and Spain was particularly concerned about its control over northern Italy, where Venice and Savoy resented Habsburg domination. A clash with Savoy over Mantua between 1613 and 1617 did not lead to a broader conflict because it was not allowed to. As we have seen, under the Duke of Lerma, Spain adopted a pacific policy, making a truce with the Dutch and a marriage alliance with the French. Indeed, the era after 1609 has been described as the *Pax Hispanica.* Lerma realised Spain could not afford the forward policy that had been adopted by Philip II (1556–1598) and sought to reorient policy concerns to the Mediterranean. However, the fall of Lerma in 1618 was to be of considerable significance for the outbreak and development of the early stages of the Thirty Years' War since his successors were to show much more concern for the fate of the King of Spain's Austrian cousin in Vienna, once problems arose. But this was a sudden, new development, not a long-term one.

2 Tensions Within the Empire

> **KEY ISSUE** What were the principal matters of dispute within the Empire?

As we have seen in the previous chapter the Peace of Augsburg was a reasonable attempt to take account of reality but it could not stop the clock. In the next quarter century and in direct contravention of the treaty, Protestantism continued to expand, so much so that by 1580 perhaps three quarters of the map of Germany had become Protestant. Still more ominous for Catholicism was the fact that even within Catholic territories large percentages of the nobility and towns had converted to Protestantism. Indeed, many felt that the old religion would be swept away, but then the Church of Rome made a remarkable comeback (known to historians as the Counter Reformation). Questions of the ownership of church property, in particular, became a constant source of conflict. Protestants wished to defend their advances; Catholics wanted 'restitution', the restoration of church lands lost since 1555. A key event in this revival was the issue of Cologne already referred to (see page 13); in late 1582 the Archbishop Elector announced he had converted to Protestantism. This was a fundamental test of the Ecclesiastical Reservation (see page 13) and of some significance for the electoral college since it would have given Protestants a majority (Saxony, Brandenburg and the Palatinate were already Protestant). A minor war ensued and the Archbishop was deposed and replaced by a Catholic. This could have provoked a major conflict, but it did not.

However, as the Catholic revival gathered steam, it led to a breakdown in the Imperial constitution. As we indicated in the last chapter, after 1601 many Protestant rulers ceased to accept the decisions of the Imperial Supreme Court (*Reichskammergericht*), but more serious still was the deadlock in the Imperial Diet (*Reichstag*). Of the seven electors in the first assembly, four were Catholic, the second assembly (the princes) tended to lean in favour of the Catholic side as well and although the third (the cities) was predominantly Protestant, it had little power. Block voting on confessional lines led to virtual paralysis by 1603, and in 1608 the Palatinate and other Protestants withdrew from the Diet in protest. A further meeting in 1613 merely confirmed this situation (see page 28). The collapse of what was a forum for compromise was not a good omen, but it was not a problem that had to be resolved by war. It just so happened that it had not been resolved when war broke out. This was simply a coincidence. Nevertheless, after the 20 year truce was signed with the Turks in 1606, the need for co-operation was removed; many German princes felt that a major war was imminent and got into considerable debt by building up their armed forces and improving fortifications. However, what is really striking about this period is that despite these tensions there was also a strong desire to avoid war. This is illustrated particularly well by two crises in Germany, the Donauwörth incident and the Cleves-Jülich affair.

a) Donauwörth 1607

Donauwörth was an imperial free city and so both Protestants (Lutherans) and Catholics had freedom of worship there. However, for some time Protestant thugs had prevented the Catholics from undertaking open worship. Accordingly in 1606 representations were made to the Emperor, Rudolf II, who ordered Maximilian of Bavaria, a champion of Counter-Reformation Catholicism (and a wily politician), to intervene. On 17th December 1607 Bavarian troops entered the city and restored Catholic worship.

Clearly this event contributed to the collapse of Protestant–Catholic cooperation in the Imperial Diet and to the formation of a Protestant military league, the Evangelical Union (both 1608). In June 1609 Maximilian was granted title to Donauwörth by the Emperor (an act of dubious legality) and he proceeded to expel the Protestants there. The following month a rival military alliance, the Catholic League, was formed. But the idea that the formation of these leagues divided Germany into two armed camps ready to go to war is false. 1618 was not 1914. The two leagues were to some extent vehicles for the ambitions of the rulers of the Palatinate and Bavaria and the conversion of Donauwörth did not herald a great Catholic offensive in Germany. In any event the Catholic League came about more as a result of another crisis, the Cleves-Jülich affair.

b) The Cleves-Jülich Affair

In 1609 the Catholic incumbent, John William, titled the Duke of Cleves-Jülich and Berg, as well as the Count of Ravensburg and Mark, died without an heir and the two claimants, Elector John Sigismund of Brandenburg, and Philip-Ludwig, Duke of Pfalz-Neuburg, were both Protestants. Accordingly, in response to the widowed Duchess and the Jülich Estates, the Emperor sent his cousin, Archduke Leopold, to take control of Jülich for the Catholics and it was immediately besieged by the claimants.

The crisis did have all the makings of an international incident as the various parties tried to recruit support outside Germany, but the assassination of Henry IV of France (May 1610) and Lerma's determination not to endanger the Truce with the Dutch meant that it did not lead to war. After the Protestant Union had successfully dislodged the Archduke Leopold from Jülich, there was no retaliation and it was decided that Cleves-Jülich would be ruled jointly by Brandenburg and Neuberg. The princes had been unnerved by the brinkmanship of

1610 and were determined to avoid war. Neuberg fell out with the Elector of Brandenburg over the condominium, but when Neuburg's son Wolfgang William converted to Catholicism in 1613 the way was open for a compromise, but not before another crisis involving Dutch and Spanish troops. Once again it was the likelihood of war that brought about a settlement, in the form of the Treaty of Xanten in November 1614.

A classic compromise was formulated: the territories were divided. Brandenburg received Cleves, Mark and Ravensburg (these territories would be Protestant), Neuburg secured Jülich and Berg (these would be Catholic). To a large extent this was facilitated by the harmony that existed between England, France and Spain at this time. In the aftermath, the Emperor Matthias and his Chancellor, Khlesl, called for the two confessional military alliances to disband. The Catholic League did so in 1617, but the Protestant Union would not; however, it pointedly only renewed its existence to 1621 (rather than for ten years) in order to avoid involvement in the Dutch–Spanish war which was expected at the expiry of the Twelve Year Truce. Once again the clear lesson of these events is the desire of the majority of rulers in Germany to avoid war at all costs.

The exception to this outlook and unmentioned thus far was the attitude of the Calvinist Elector Palatine, Frederick V, or more particularly his Chancellor, Christian, Prince of Anhalt-Bernburg, who consistently sought to undermine Habsburg authority (by links with the Protestant Estates in Austria for instance) and saw Cleves-Jülich as a greater defeat than Donauwörth. But Anhalt was gearing up for a major war in 1621; he did not foresee the Bohemian revolt.

What these two crises demonstrate is that although there were significant tensions in the Empire, compromise and the wish to avoid war could keep the peace. These events were not causes of the Thirty Years' War. The Thirty Years' War emanated from an internal Habsburg problem, a revolt in Bohemia.

3 Tensions in the *Erbländer*

> **KEY ISSUE** What issues led to the Bohemian revolt?

a) A House Divided

The idea that the Catholic advance was in some way a manifestation of the triumph of Imperial despotism (tyranny) over princely particularism (autonomy) as some Protestant contemporaries and even some later historians have contended, is a myth. The Austrian Habsburgs, and the Emperor in particular, were in fact very weak at this time. As we have seen, the Austrian branch of the family had not done well when the territories of Charles V were divided and what weakened the Austrian branch even more was the tripartite division of Ferdinand's lands at his death in 1564. This became even more complicated by the end of the century, when there was a fourfold division: Upper Austria was ruled by Archduke Matthias as Governor from Vienna, and the Emperor, Rudolf II, ruled Lower Austria, Bohemia (and its dependencies) and Hungary from Prague. Archduke Ferdinand succeeded his father in Styria, and Maximilian's son, Archduke Maximilian, ruled in the Tyrol.

Moreover, as we have seen, two further developments undermined Habsburg authority: one was the establishment of representative assemblies dominated by the aristocracy in all the Austrian duchies, and the other was the growth of Protestantism within these lands. By 1580 some 90 per cent of the nobles in Upper and Lower Austria were Protestant and the Catholic presence was equally weak in Bohemia and Hungary. Given the Habsburgs' commitment to Catholicism, this was clearly a recipe for disaster. The situation was further complicated by the personality of the Emperor, Rudolf II. An odd character, he became increasingly withdrawn and unstable as time went on so that from about 1600 a political vacuum began to appear at the head of the family. This led to the intervention of his siblings, the Archdukes, from 1605, but this in turn created even more problems.

b) Matthias vs. Rudolf

At the beginning of the seventeenth century Emperor Rudolf II, despite his unpredictable nature, showed some determination to recover lost ground for Catholicism, but this jeopardised the war effort against the Turks (1593–1606) since it led to revolt in Hungary. The other archdukes were naturally alarmed at their brother's lack of political sense and increasingly erratic behaviour, and therefore decided (in 1605) to authorise Matthias to settle with the Hungarians and Turkey, which he duly did (1606), but at the price of religious toleration.

Subsequently in 1608 Rudolf was deposed as King of Hungary and Matthias elected in his place. Now the Protestants in the Austrian Estates led by George Tschernembl demanded full religious liberty and Matthias felt constrained to grant this too, in 1609. Only Bohemia, Silesia and Lusatia remained under Rudolf's direct rule and in 1609 here also religious liberty was secured. Rudolf was obliged to sign the Letter of Majesty on 9th July 1609. It stated:

> 1 ... in respect of the faiths of one or both kinds ... no man shall vex another, but rather ... all shall hold together as good friends ... Furthermore ... We do will and particularly enjoin that, for the preservation of amity and concord, each party shall practise its religion
> 5 freely and without restriction, subject to the governance and direction

of its own clergy and that neither party shall impose any rules on the other in respect of its religion or usages, neither prevent the practice of its religion, internment of bodies in churches or graveyards, or tolling of bells ... As from today, no person, neither of the higher free Estates
10 nor the inhabitants of unfree towns and villages, nor the peasants, shall be forced or compelled by any device by the authorities over them or by any person, spiritual or temporal, to forsake his religion and accept another religion.[1]

This granted Bohemians the right to choose between Catholicism and various non-Catholic faiths – Utraquist (Hussite), Bohemian Brethren, or Lutheran. It also gave them the right to build schools and churches, and a standing committee of the Estates, the 'Defensors', was established to ensure the Letter was enforced. Indeed, the 'Defensors' became virtual co-regents.

Two years later Rudolf seems to have had second thoughts and tried to reverse the concessions by force (and fight his brother), but he was unsuccessful. The Defensors called upon Matthias to take over and Rudolf was declared deposed. In May 1611, Matthias, having confirmed the Letter of Majesty, was crowned King of Bohemia. As Geoffrey Parker has put it, 'the Power of the Estates in the Habsburg lands had rarely seemed so great.'[2] However, the growth of Protestant rights represented a considerable political challenge to the sovereignty and power of the Catholic Habsburg rulers, and one which Matthias, despite having obtained power by making concessions, could not allow to continue.

c) The Emperor Matthias (1612–19)

Emperor Rudolf II died a broken man in 1612 and was succeeded to his title by Matthias in the same year. The new Emperor faced two significant problems: he had to re-establish his authority at the expense of the Protestant Estates and he had to designate an heir. He was not young (55), in poor health and childless, and the most obvious candidates to succeed him were Philip III of Spain and Archduke Ferdinand of Styria. The former despite a better claim was inclined to concede to the latter in return for concessions. Jesuit-educated Ferdinand was the choice of hard-line Catholics; Matthias, on the other hand, was not. In his youth he had flirted with Protestantism and it was felt (quite justifiably) that his struggle with the ineffectual Rudolf had enabled the Protestants to benefit. However, it made sense for him now to throw in his lot with the Catholic hardliners if he was going to reduce the political power of the Protestants.

Within the Empire Matthias and his chancellor, Khlesl, adopted a conciliatory policy as they wished to establish a united front in the face of the renewed Turkish threat. Although the Diet of 1613 was unsuccessful in restoring the authority of Imperial institutions, there is no doubt that the resolution of the Cleves Jülich affair in 1614 and the dissolution of the Catholic League in 1617 (see page 26) did reduce the tension. However, within the Habsburg dominions a more hard-line approach was adopted. At the Linz and Prague Diets in 1614 and 1615 the Emperor was able to take advantage of divisions to obtain new taxes and transfer some of the public debts. However, to some extent the more hard-line approach was initiated by others. In Bohemia, for instance, the Archbishop of Prague ordered the closure of a Protestant church at Klostergrab (in 1614) and forced the citizens to attend Catholic services. The following year the Emperor responded by not only confirming the closure but by closing another at Braunau. By the end of 1616 a large number of Catholic incumbents had prohibited Protestant worship in direct contravention of the Letter of Majesty. Clearly a major crisis was looming. However, what actually proved decisive for this crisis, and for the outbreak of the war, was the adoption of Archduke Ferdinand of Styria as Matthias's successor in 1617.

d) Archduke Ferdinand of Styria

Ferdinand turned out to be the arch-exponent of Counter Reformation Catholicism. But what exactly was Counter Reformation Catholicism? The Counter Reformation is in reality only a historian's label and its validity has been called into question in recent years. However, for our purposes it can be defined as both a process of change and renewal within Catholicism and as an aggressive attack on the Protestant Reformation. It manifested itself in the conversion of important persons, a revival of monastic life, the recovery of ecclesiastical territory from Protestants, and the suppression of Protestant worship. Its most aggressive arm was the Society of Jesus founded by Ignatius Loyola in 1540. Jesuits, as they were known, were active in education and conversion and enjoyed considerable influence as confessors to princes and kings. One such prince was Archduke Ferdinand of Styria. Up to this point the Catholic revival had made only piecemeal progress mainly independent of the Habsburgs; now with Ferdinand at the helm it would become official policy.

Ferdinand was born in Graz in 1578 and he attended the Jesuit university of Ingolstadt from 1590 to 1595 (see the Profile on page 38). Although personally easy-going the Archduke, as he became in 1596, was very much under the influence of his advisers. Soon after becoming ruler of Inner Austria (Styria, Carinthia, Carniola) he set out to suppress Protestantism by forcing the great majority of his subjects to adopt the Catholic faith and by expelling those who would not (perhaps as many as 5,000 in number).

After the election of Matthias the Archdukes agreed that the succession to the Imperial title was between Ferdinand and Philip III of Spain. Philip was prepared to concede at a price, but initially negotiations made little headway. However, from 1615 Ferdinand found himself involved in the Uzkok War (see glossary) and he was happy to negotiate with Spain in return for financial aid. The Oñate Treaty (actually the Treaty of Graz), so-called after the Spanish ambassador, was signed on March 20th 1617 and ratified in July. In return for Spanish recognition as heir to Matthias and one million thalers in cash, Ferdinand agreed to cede Finale Ligura and Piombino (already in Spanish hands) and parts of Alsace (which were never handed over). This did not as yet represent a dramatic change in Spanish policy. Zúñiga, a former ambassador to Prague and an advocate of cooperation with the Austrian branch of the Habsburg family, did not join the Council of State in Madrid until July 1617 and the triumph of his policy over that of Lerma only occurred during 1618 after the outbreak of the war (and as a response to it).

Matthias, feeling that he was at death's door, decided to move fast and on June 17th 1617 he persuaded the Bohemians to accept Ferdinand as king-designate. The Protestants were caught off guard without an alternative candidate and the Catholic Crown officials led by Chancellor Lobkowitz pushed the election through. When the Protestants recovered, all they could do was get Ferdinand to agree to respect the Letter of Majesty, but clearly they had been outwitted. He was crowned on July 19th and the Emperor and King proceeded to Dresden in August to obtain the goodwill of the Elector of Saxony, John George. The Emperor subsequently summoned the Hungarian Diet and Ferdinand was recognised as king there the following year (though not without some debate). The pair spent most of the winter in Vienna leaving Prague in December in the hands of a committee of ten regents, seven of whom were Catholic. In a country where 90 per cent of the people were non-Catholic, this was not designed to create harmony. Moreover, acting on orders from Ferdinand the regents passed a number of provocative measures. Payment for Protestants from Catholic endowments was suspended; a censorship of all printed matter was established; and non-Catholics were barred from civic office. However, the issue that proved the catalyst was the festering problem of the Protestant churches in Braunau and Klostergrab. The latter was actually pulled down and the burgers of the former were arrested for objecting to an order requiring them to give up their church.

This offensive against the Protestants generated considerable fear among all non-Catholics and naturally led the Defensors of the Letter of Majesty to summon a meeting of the Estates in Prague on March 5th 1618, where Count Thurn, their leader, demanded the immediate release of the Braunau prisoners. Matthias rejected their petition and required them to disperse, which they did. However, they met again in May, but were once again told to disperse. This time they did not. Instead on May 23rd 1618 they marched to the Hradschin Palace and hurled two Catholic Regents, Martinitz and Slavata, and their secretary, out of the window. The three landed on a dung heap and survived, which the Catholics interpreted as a good omen. A contemporary account reflects this feeling:

1   Four members of the Estate of Lords and one knight forcibly laid hands on the count of Martinitz, held him down and led him to the opened window whilst shouting: 'Now we will take our just revenge on our religious enemies.' When Martinitz understood the nature of his impend-
5   ing death, he loudly called out: 'Since I must now die for God, His Holy Catholic Faith and His Royal Majesty, I will put up with anything but only allow me to see my confessor so that I can confess my sins.' Those gentlemen who were present only gave him the following reply: 'We will now send a villainous Jesuit to join you.' Whilst Count Martinitz was
10 highly troubled at this and sincerely beginning to repent his sins, the above persons lifted him off the ground and cast him head first out of the window into the depth of the castle moat. As he fell, he called out the names of Jesus and Mary, and he landed so gently on the ground that it was as if his plea to the Virgin Mary and the protection of God
15 during his terrible fall saved him from all harm despite his corpulent body. Several devout and trustworthy people have also affirmed that they saw the most serene Virgin Mary catch the gentleman in the air with her cloak and carry him to earth.[3]

This 'Defenestration of Prague', as it was called, marked the beginning of the Thirty Years' War. Of course there had been rebellions in Bohemia before, as recently as 1609 and 1611, but what made this different was the fact that Ferdinand was not prepared to compromise, particularly as he had Spanish backing. Accordingly the Protestants were forced to depose him and seek a new king from the Palatinate. Thus although the war began as an internal Habsburg problem, from the start it had international implications that could turn it into a wider conflict. However, it was the intransigence of Ferdinand (and the determination of the Protestant nobles of Bohemia to stem the Catholic revival and maintain their supremacy) that ensured there would be no settlement.

This event when it occurred took Europe by surprise, a fact which to some extent belies any attempt by historians to give primacy of place to long-term causes. Yet from this distance we can see that the growth of Protestantism in the Habsburg hereditary territories represented not only a challenge to Catholicism but also a challenge to Habsburg political sovereignty. The conjunction of a Catholic revival with the determined policy of Ferdinand and a subsequent change of policy in Madrid ensured that a showdown would occur. That a Bohemian rebellion would spark off a Thirty Years' War, however, is something no contemporary could have foreseen, but then no one could have foreseen that the Habsburgs would go on to enjoy such complete success – in the initial phases at least.

4 Conclusion

Thomas Munck recently stated: 'it is certainly indisputable that no simple explanation of [the] causes ... of the Thirty Years War can do justice to what was in fact a composite and at times highly disjointed conflict'.[4] While there is clearly some truth in this, students should be aware that we are here concerned with the outbreak of a war that became known as the Thirty Years' War; we are not concerned with why a war broke out that lasted thirty years – in this chapter at least. The length of the war had more to do with how events unfolded than how it started. Clearly once conflict broke out, all the other tensions in the Empire – the religious divide, the Catholic revival, constitutional paralysis, fear of Imperial absolutism etc. – coalesced with all the other European tensions. – Baltic rivalry, Dutch and French opposition to Spanish power etc. – to create a war that went on and on until all these problems, which were running in parallel, were to some extent resolved. Nevertheless, it has been the thesis of this chapter that short-term causes were paramount in setting off the conflict. That is not to deny that there were long-term causes, and these would need some mention in an essay on this topic. Clearly if the Augsburg Treaty and the divisions of the Habsburg lands in the 1550s are relevant, then can we not also argue the same for the Reformation and Counter-Reformation? Some mention of the religious divide and Austrian Habsburg weakness is essential, but the key factors remain the growth of 'political' Protestantism in Austria and Bohemia in 1608–9 and the Catholic backlash which gained full momentum with the choice of Ferdinand of Styria as Matthias's heir in 1617. At the beginning of the war, then, the issue was Austrian Habsburg power, be it in terms of political or religious authority; and remarkably this remained the central theme throughout the war, initially as a matter of its weakness, later one of its apparent strength – despite the influence of other tensions and conflicts.

References

1 Quoted in C.A. Macartney (ed.), *The Habsburg and Hohenzollern Dynasties in the 17th and 18th Centuries* (Macmillan, 1970), pp. 22–30.
2 G. Parker (ed.), *The Thirty Years' War* (Routledge, 1984), p. 11.
3 Quoted in G. Benecke, *Germany in the Thirty Years' War* (Arnold, 1978), p. 12.
4 Thomas Munck, *Seventeenth Century Europe* (Macmillan, 1990), p. 2.

Summary Diagram
Tensions in Europe

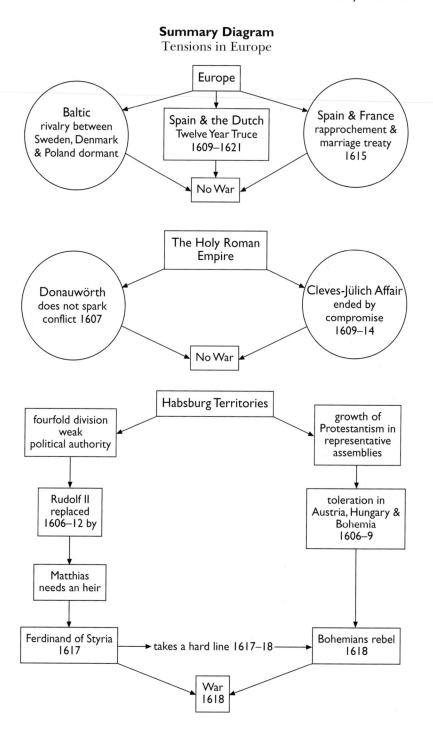

Answering essay questions on Chapter 2

It should be noted that many questions that refer to the causes might encompass other aspects of the war, thus '"Confused in its causes, futile in its results". Is this a fair description of the Thirty Years' War?' Or 'To what extent did the Peace of Westphalia resolve the causes of the war? Or '"Originally religious, latterly political". How far do you agree with this assessment of the Thirty Years' War?' However, in this section we are only concerned with those questions that are solely about the war's origins.

Consider the following questions:

1. 'The Peace of Augsburg by its recognition of the principle of *cuius regio, eius religio* within Germany sowed the seeds of future conflict.' Does this statement provide an adequate explanation of the outbreak of The Thirty Years War?
2. 'Catholic militants caused the Thirty Years War.' Discuss.
3. Were the causes of the outbreak of war in the Holy Roman Empire in 1618 political rather than religious?

You should use your introduction in your essay to address the question, define its terms where necessary and begin to answer it by explaining your view. The rest of the essay should then be used to justify the position you have taken at the beginning by developing the argument with relevant factual support. Remember that the greatest enemy of the effective essay is irrelevance: hence you should be addressing the question at all times, not necessarily always explicitly but certainly implicitly. By the time you reach your conclusion you should have the marks in the bag.

The first question explicitly requires you to consider long-term factors, going back to 1555. Thus you would need to look at how Augsburg worked for a while until the Catholic revival led to growing confrontation and a breakdown in the Imperial constitution. Naturally enough consideration of the religious divide alone, a problem that undoubtedly had to be resolved, would not be 'an adequate explanation of the outbreak of the Thirty Years War', since the war did not begin in Germany. You would need to go on to consider the parallel crisis in the Habsburg lands: the weakness of Habsburg government in the face of the Protestant advance, compounded by Rudolf II's poor mental and physical health. Finally you would have to focus on events in Bohemia and the Imperial succession, and refer back to Augsburg since religious differences did play a central role throughout. In the course of the essay mention might be made of other European tensions, if only to point out that Europe was remarkably peaceful during the second decade of the seventeenth century.

The second question suggests you blame the hardline Catholics (Ferdinand in particular) and it would be wise to include a paragraph on what Counter-Reformation Catholicism was and how it manifested itself (see page 29). However, if you then go on to discuss what actually happenened in the later years of Rudolf II's reign, you will notice that the Protestants are making considerable headway in the territories under Habsburg direct rule. Because of this Ferdinand decided to strike back. So who is to blame? You should focus on Bohemia rather than Germany, pointing out that this is where the war started. Naturally you will also need to explain the religious divide and Austrian Habsburg weakness.

The third question requires you to run through most of the same material but it also requires you to distinguish between religion and politics, two elements which, we are often told, were so inextricably intertwined in this period that it is almost impossible to distinguish between them; and yet this is the war in which politics, *raison d'état* (literally, reason of state – that is to say, putting the interests of the state before anything else), triumphed over religion. Whatever you decide, it is important to remember that the majority of people who lived through the conflict saw it in religious terms, and even those politicians who cynically manipulated religion for political ends used religious terminology to disguise that fact. If it is any help, one thing we can say is that genuine religious motives loomed larger at the beginning of the conflict than at the end (see Chapter 7).

Of course it is possible to suggest, quite legitimately, that the causes were both political and religious. After all the Protestants in Austria and Bohemia wanted freedom of worship, but by obtaining this through the Estates the nobles had strengthened their political role. Similarly Ferdinand genuinely wished to re-establish Catholicism but at the same time the growth of 'political' Protestantism threatened Habsburg political sovereignty and undermined his authority. He had to do something about it. Clearly religion and politics were intertwined at the beginning of the conflict.

3 The Habsburgs Triumphant 1618–29

POINTS TO CONSIDER

This chapter will look at the failure of the Bohemian Revolt, the continuation of the war, the failure of Danish intervention and the issuing of the Edict of Restitution. Your aim should be to understand why the Habsburgs were so successful, why despite their success the war did not come to an end and why the Emperor Ferdinand threw away what seemed to be such a strong position.

KEY DATES

1618	**May**	Defenestration of Prague
	Oct	Fall of Lerma
1619	**March**	Death of Matthias
	Aug	Deposition of Ferdinand
		Election of Frederick V as king of Bohemia
		Ferdinand II elected Emperor
	Oct	Treaty of Munich
1620	**March**	Mülhausen Guarantee
	July	Treaty of Ulm: Catholic League occupies upper Austria
	Aug	Spinola invades Rhine Palatinate
	Nov	Battle of White Mountain
1621	**April**	War between Spain and Dutch resumes
	May	Evangelical Union dissolves
	Oct	Catholic League occupies Upper Palatinate
1622	**May**	Battle of Wimpfen
	June	Battle of Höchst
	Autumn	Catholic League occupies rest of Rhine Palatinate
1623	**Feb**	Palatine Electorate transferred to Maximilian of Bavaria
	Aug	Battle of Stadtlohn
1624	**Aug**	Cardinal Richelieu becomes chief minister of France
1625	**April**	Christian IV elected *Kreisoberst* of Lower Saxon Circle
	July	Wallenstein raises new Imperial army
1626	**April**	Battle of Dessau Bridge
	Aug	Battle of Lutter
1627	**from Feb**	Wallenstein overruns mainland Denmark and northern Germany
	Sept	Revised Constitution for Bohemia and Moravia
1628	**Jan**	Wallenstein becomes Duke of Mecklenburg
	May	Bavaria annexes Upper Palatinate
	May–July	Unsuccessful siege of Stralsund
	Sept	Battle of Wolgast
1629	**March**	Edict of Restitution

July	Peace of Lübeck
1630 July	Gustavus Adolphus lands in Germany
July–Nov	Regensburg Electoral Meeting
Aug	Wallenstein dismissed

1 The Bohemian Revolt and the Palatine War 1618–23

> **KEY ISSUE** Why did the rebels fail and why, despite their defeat, did the war go on?

a) Events

The Defenestration of Prague was not as spontaneous as it might seem. It was a rather belated response to the stage-managed adoption of Ferdinand of Styria as king-designate and an attempt to re-establish the superiority of the Protestant Estates prior to Matthias's death. There was little room for compromise; the Bohemian nobles had thrown down the gauntlet – and Ferdinand was not the sort of man to make a deal. This was both a strength and a weakness: a weakness in the sense that he had no conception of the seriousness of his situation – soon most of the hereditary lands were in revolt and he had no means of preventing this development; and a strength in the sense that he was so convinced of the rightness of his position that he showed considerable determination in the face of adversity and ultimately was able to triumph (in the matter of the hereditary lands at least).

Initially the revolt prospered. In the summer of 1618 Lusatia, Silesia and Upper Austria joined Bohemia and in the summer of 1619 so did Moravia and Lower Austria (see the map on page 39). There was little hope of a settlement: Ferdinand actually removed Cardinal Khlesl, Matthias' main adviser, who was thought to favour a deal, and with the death of Matthias in March 1619 what little hope there had been of a compromise settlement was gone.

In the summer of 1619 the rebels under Count Thurn actually besieged Vienna for a time as they did again later that year with the aid of Bethlen Gabor, the prince of Transylvania, who had joined the rebels and overrun Hungary. In August the Bohemians formally deposed Ferdinand and on August 26th offered the crown to Frederick V, the Elector of the Palatinate. After much soul searching and against the advice of almost everyone (including his father-in-law, James I of England), he accepted on September 28th. It proved to be a fateful decision.

In the meantime Ferdinand was hanging on with grim determination. Initially he owed his survival to the initiative of the Spanish

EMPEROR FERDINAND II (1578–1637)

-Profile-

Ferdinand was born in Graz and became Archduke of Styria in 1590. Educated at the Jesuit University of Ingolstadt, Ferdinand proved to be something of a Catholic zealot. The rector of the university stated: 'nothing sown in this fertile soil seems to perish', and Cardinal Khlesl, Matthias' adviser, complained: 'the court of Graz is ruled as much by the counsel of the Jesuits as by that of his advisers'. As Archduke of Styria he had over 5,000 Protestants expelled in 1599–1600 and when he became Matthias' heir and designate of Bohemia in 1617 he moved swiftly to place Catholics in positions of authority. Indeed because of these moves he bears some responsibility for the outbreak of the war in 1618. On becoming Emperor in 1619 he went on to triumph, defeating the Bohemian rebels by 1620, the Elector Palatine by 1623, and the king of Denmark by 1629. In that year he issued the Edict of Restitution, the logical culmination of both his success and his devotion to Catholicism. However, his decision to sacrifice Wallenstein, his general in 1630, left him unprepared to face the king of Sweden, Gustavus Adolphus, in the same year. Although Ferdinand was able to recover some lost ground with Spanish aid after Gustavus' death, he was unable to achieve a lasting peace in 1635 (the Peace of Prague). Despite Ferdinand sacrificing the Edict and taking a more political and less religious approach, the war was still far from over when he died in 1637.

Contemporaries formed very diverse judgments of Ferdinand. To some he was friendly and mild mannered but to others he was tough and inflexible, the arch-exponent of Counter Reformation Catholicism. Although not a complete success there is no doubt that he revived the fortunes of the Habsburg Monarchy and laid the foundations for the later success of the Austrian branch.

ambassador, Count Oñate, who was able to raise loans and persuade Madrid to come to Ferdinand's aid with both money and men. After weathering the initial storm Ferdinand's position began to improve. On August 28th 1619 he was unanimously elected Emperor in succession to Matthias and in October he signed the Treaty of Munich with Spain and Maximilian of Bavaria. Encouraged by Spanish

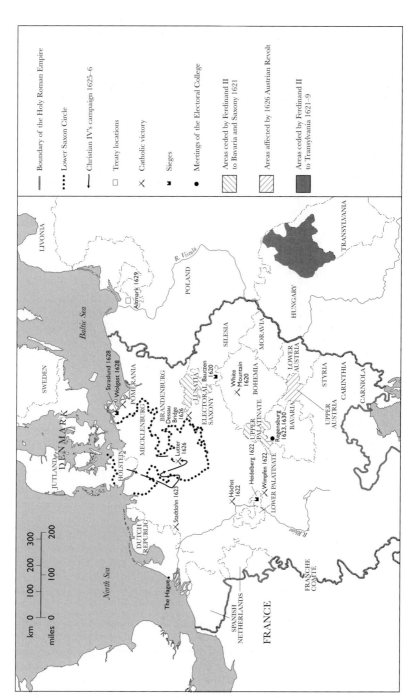

Legend

— Boundary of the Holy Roman Empire
•••• Lower Saxon Circle
→ Christian IV's campaign 1625–6
□ Treaty locations
✕ Catholic victory
▪ Sieges
• Meetings of the Electoral College
▨ Areas ceded by Ferdinand II to Bavaria and Saxony 1621
▨ Areas affected by 1626 Austrian Revolt
▨ Areas ceded by Ferdinand II to Transylvania 1621–9

The war 1618–29

(Map labels:)

LIVONIA
SWEDEN
Baltic Sea
North Sea
JUTLAND
DENMARK
POLAND
R. Vistula
Altmark 1629 □
Stralsund 1628 ▪
Wolgast 1628 ✕
POMERANIA
MECKLENBURG
HOLSTEIN
Stadtlohn 1623 ✕
BRANDENBURG
Dessau Bridge 1626 ✕
Lutter 1626 ✕
SILESIA
LUSATIA
Bautzen 1620 ▪
ELECTORAL SAXONY
White Mountain 1620 ✕
BOHEMIA
MORAVIA
HUNGARY
TRANSYLVANIA
LOWER AUSTRIA
UPPER AUSTRIA
UPPER PALATINATE
Regensburg 1623,1630 •
BAVARIA
STYRIA
CARINTHIA
CARNIOLA
Heidelberg 1622 ▪
Wimpfen 1622 ✕
Höchst 1622 ✕
LOWER PALATINATE
R. Rhine
DUTCH REPUBLIC
The Hague •
SPANISH NETHERLANDS
FRANCE
FRANCHE COMTÉ

Scale

km 0 100 200 300
miles 0 100 200

support, Maximilian had reconstituted the Catholic League and was now able to offer Ferdinand military support in return for a very favourable deal. In the event of complete success Ferdinand promised Maximilian, verbally at first, Frederick's territory of the Upper Palatinate[1] and Frederick's electoral title, though in all probability the Emperor did not expect complete success and did not expect to have to make these transfers.

In 1620 the tide turned. In January a truce was made with Bethlen Gabor and in March the electors met at Mülhausen to reassure the Protestants of northern and eastern Germany that the Catholic League would not try to regain former ecclesiastical possessions. This prevented the war from spreading. Out of the Mülhausen Guarantee (20 March 1620) came an agreement with the Lutheran elector John George of Saxony, who agreed to support Ferdinand in return for the territory of Lusatia and continuing toleration in Bohemia, Silesia and Moravia. Although a Protestant, John George had no wish to see his rival Frederick, a Calvinist, retain the throne of Bohemia.

This meeting also led ultimately to the Neutrality Pact at Ulm in July 1620 whereby the (Protestant) Evangelical Union and the Catholic League agreed not to attack each other. This effectively neutralised the Protestants and ensured that the war would be confined to the Habsburg dominions (in fact the Evangelical Union dissolved itself the following year, May 1621). This left the Catholics free to suppress the revolt and in the same month 30,000 Catholic League troops overran Upper Austria while an Imperial army took Lower Austria and John George took Lusatia. In August Spinola occupied the western half of the Rhine Palatinate with Spanish troops. Subsequently the Imperial and Catholic League armies joined together, marched into Bohemia and won a decisive battle at White Mountain near Prague on 8th November. The Bohemian Revolt was effectively over and Frederick fled to the Dutch Republic.

Bohemia was now subjected to savage repression. The leaders who had not fled were executed, Protestantism was suppressed and over 750 noble families suffered partial or full confiscation of their estates. By 1627–8 the whole nobility faced the choice of either conversion or exile. It is estimated that over 30,000 people left Bohemia in 1627, and that the overall population fell by 50 per cent between 1615 and 1650. In addition the Bohemian monarchy was made hereditary in the House of Habsburg and was given enhanced authority, as this extract from the Revised Constitution issued in May 1627 makes clear:

1 We, Ferdinand, hereby make known to all and sundry since we have, with the help and support of Almighty God, reconquered Our Hereditary Kingdom of Bohemia with the power of the sword and reduced it to obedience to our authority, we have made it our chief
5 purpose to secure that the honour of Almighty God be established in this Hereditary Kingdom and that fitting justice – yet not untempered

by the mercifulness natural to us and with moderation of its full rigour
– be meted out to those who revolted against us, for an example to
others and to avert the most injurious consequences, not for ourselves
10 alone but for all princes. Since, now, all this has taken place, we have
duly considered how the said kingdom shall be restored to a condition
in which the subjects' respect and obedience to us and our heirs shall
be assured, the subjects jointly administered in peace, calm, and unity
under the protection of an impartial law and uniform religion, and
15 everything that is contrary to this abolished.

Although Ferdinand did hand over Lusatia to John George of Saxony
he ignored the promise of continuing toleration. Re-Catholicisation
occurred throughout the reconquered hereditary territories though
it was not a rapid process. Protestants could be expelled and their
churches pulled down but it took a long time to build up a new
Catholic infrastructure.

The Bohemian Revolt may have been over but the Palatine War
went on. Frederick still had a few allies in that area, minor princes
whom the Dutch were prepared to fund. Count Ernst von Mansfeld,
who had fought for Frederick in Bohemia, was able to raise an army,
as did George Frederick of Baden and Christian of Brunswick.
However, Count Jean Tilly, who commanded the Catholic League
army, was able to occupy the Upper Palatinate in 1621 and went on to
defeat the Protestants in separate battles in 1622 – George Frederick
at Wimpfen (6 May) and Christian at Höchst (20 June). This left
Mansfeld in an impossible position; he retreated and the way was left
open for Tilly to occupy the eastern half of the Rhine Palatinate.
Accordingly Heidelberg fell in September 1622. In 1623 Frederick
did manage to assemble another army, again with Dutch financial
support, but Tilly quickly moved North and inflicted a total defeat on
Christian of Brunswick at Stadtlohn near the Dutch border on August
6th. The Palatine War was effectively over.

Earlier, in February at the Electoral Diet of Regensburg, Ferdinand
had officially transferred Frederick's electoral title to Maximilian of
Bavaria, but due to opposition this was granted to him for his lifetime
only. Maximilian continued to occupy both Upper Austria and the
Upper Palatinate pending a settlement of his expenses. Finally following a major revolt in Upper Austria in 1626, it was decided in 1628
that the Elector of Bavaria would 'buy' the Upper Palatinate for the
price of the Emperor's debt to him and evacuate Upper Austria, which
he duly did. So, it would appear that Ferdinand and the Catholic
League had been totally successful. The war should have been over.

b) Analysis

Principally there are three questions to ask about this first episode of
the war:

i) Why did the rebels fail?

It is clear that the rebels failed because they were unable to gain sufficient support from both inside and outside the Empire. One of the reasons the rebels picked Frederick of the Palatinate to be their new king was because of his familial connections[2] but this proved to be misguided. The German princes' willingness to accept the Mülhausen Guarantee and the Ulm treaty reflected their earnest desire to avoid war at all costs. As already mentioned Frederick's father-in-law, James I, disapproved of his actions and sought to achieve an overarching diplomatic settlement by means of a deal with Spain. Moreover at the same time the other Protestant powers were unavailable to assist – the Swedes were more concerned about the Poles, and the Dutch, initially torn apart by an internal dispute between the Advocate of Holland and Maurice of Nassau of the House of Orange, were preoccupied with the end of the Twelve Year Truce with Spain which led to a renewal of the war in 1621. France too was not prepared to assist. Louis XIII, unlike his father Henry IV, was not really sympathetic to Protestants and it was French mediation that brokered the Treaty of Ulm and the consequent emasculation of the Evangelical Union. Without French support the German protestant princes could not contemplate any involvement in the war. In any event for the western Protestant powers Bohemia was just too far geographically removed for easy intervention.

So, apart from Bethlen Gabor, the Prince of Transylvania, who proved to be an intermittent ally, the rebels were unable to generate any substantial outside support – which, as it turned out, was going to be essential for them to succeed.

In addition, the revolt itself had inherent weaknesses: it was essentially a noble revolt and had little popular support. The nobles feared the peasants, they feared social upheaval and for this reason they relied entirely on securing foreign aid which, as we have noted, they were unable to obtain. It is also hard to see where the revolt could eventually lead without some agreement with the Emperor – and at no time was that forthcoming.

ii) How did Ferdinand triumph?

In 1618 Ferdinand was in an extremely weak position with no forces of his own. As we have already suggested, his determination was undoubtedly a factor in his success – a lesser man might have made some sort of deal, but of principal importance was the fact that he, unlike the rebels, was able to call upon outside assistance. Spanish aid in particular was fundamental at the beginning of the conflict and although initially it was at the behest of the ambassador Count Oñate, subsequently, with the fall of the pacific Duke of Lerma at the end of 1618 and the rise of Don Balthasar de Zúñiga, it became a matter of Spanish policy.[3] Vast sums of money – 6 million thalers by the end of 1624 – were despatched and large numbers of troops: 7,000 in 1619 rising to 12,000 in 1620, these forming the basis of the Imperial army. In addition, the Spanish sent Spinola with a further 20,000 troops to assist in the Rhine Palatinate. Ferdinand was also able to secure the support of Maximilian of Bavaria and the reconstituted Catholic League – albeit at a high price – as well as John George of Saxony and the Pope who gave substantial financial backing. Moreover, his unchallenged election as Emperor in August 1619 gave him immense political authority and presented the rebels with serious legal difficulties. Both the Bohemians and the Elector Palatine had hoped for a postponement of the election pending a full resolution of the crisis. However, they were to be sadly mistaken and both the Bohemians and Frederick went on to suffer complete defeat. This then begs the third question.

iii) Why did the war not come to an end in 1623?

It could be argued that an extension of the conflict would have been far less likely had Ferdinand been able to deal with the rebellion himself. Clearly his weakness internationalised the conflict and made him beholden to both Spain and Maximilian of Bavaria. Of course by electing Frederick of the Palatinate the rebels too had taken the conflict beyond the bounds of the Habsburg hereditory territories, but clearly Ferdinand's transfer of Frederick's electoral territory and title to Maximilian caused considerable unease, and to many suggested a somewhat high-handed Imperial approach. Moreover the fate of Frederick V was left unresolved. What is certainly true and what is crucial is the fact that Ferdinand's success was so complete that the balance of power in the Holy Roman Empire had now changed dramatically. The Emperor had in effect been too successful, as indeed had the Catholic League which now had a large army in northern Germany. From 1624 onwards, Protestant powers outside the Empire began to get involved to try to redress the balance, and this is why the war went on. In particular the Dutch Republic, England and Denmark came together in an alliance that was both anti-Habsburg and anti-Catholic. Thus from 1624 the conflict became increasingly internationalised, ever more complex and bafflingly intricate – baffingly intricate because of the large number of repudiated negotiations and unratified treaties which make it difficult to unravel. Of course Frederick had received Dutch funding throughout and in many ways the Dutch Republic is an important link between the first and second phases of the war; however, it is important to remember that the war between Spain and the Dutch (that had restarted in 1621) and the war in Germany remained by and large two distinct conflicts. Indeed it was to be Denmark which gave its name to the next phase, not the Dutch Republic.

2 The Danish Episode 1625–9

KEY ISSUE Why did Christian IV intervene and why did he fail?

After the Spanish marriage fiasco in 1623[4] English policy changed quite dramatically. Although James I remained cautious, he did decide to subsidise a joint Anglo-French force led by Mansfeld and, together with the Dutch and Brandenburg, decided to invite Gustavus Adolphus, the king of Sweden, to intervene on Frederick's behalf. However, the negotiations were tortuous and Gustavus' demands proved to be too great: he refused to co-operate with the French, who were by now rather concerned about Habsburg success, and he demanded full command of all the armies. These developments alarmed Gustavus' arch-rival, Christian IV, king of Denmark, who feared an expansion of Swedish power into Germany. Accordingly in January 1625 he offered to intervene himself. Indeed he did intervene early in 1625 without securing support from anyone – even his own council was opposed to intervention (he did, however, have independent financial means).[5] Of course he had his own reasons for doing so. As the Duke of Holstein he was already a 'German Prince' and his principal aim was to extend his influence in the Lower Saxon Circle – indeed he was elected its military commander *(kreisoberst)* in April 1625. Nevertheless, Christian did not lose sight of the overall cause – he pledged to restore Frederick to the Palatinate and he styled himself Defender of the Protestant Faith, but personal ambition seems to have loomed large in his calculations. The military encounters of 1625 proved inconclusive but at the end of the year Christian IV did finally achieve an alliance. This was the Hague Convention (9 December) – the English and Dutch pledged to finance the campaign and place the forces of Mansfeld and Christian of Brunswick under his overall command. But that was the extent of the anti-Habsburg alliance. Gustavus Adolphus was now out of the picture as he resumed his war with Poland in 1625 (and Brandenburg declared neutrality because of this). France too no longer took an active role as internal Huguenot (French protestant) problems came to dominate the policy of the new French first minister, Cardinal Richelieu.

Moreover, if that was not bad enough, the alliance itself had inherent weaknesses. English support proved to be a damp squib. Charles I, who succeeded James in 1625, did not have the finances to fulfill the treaty obligations and in any event got involved in war with Spain (1625–30) and subsequently France (1627–9). Given these factors and Charles' difficulties with Parliament it is not surprising that England played a largely insignificant role in the conflict hereafter.

However, this was not Christian's major problem. During the course of 1625 and at the behest of Maximilian of Bavaria, who was concerned about Danish ambitions, the Emperor Ferdinand had been encouraged to finally raise an army of his own (he could no longer rely on Spain which was now too preoccupied with the Dutch to lend any support were it to be needed.). So, he entrusted supreme command to a Czech (Bohemian) nobleman, Albrecht von Wallenstein. As a Catholic, Wallenstein had benefitted enormously from the destruction of the Protestant elite in Bohemia and had acquired vast estates by purchasing confiscated land. Indeed it has been estimated that he might have owned about a quarter of the entire kingdom of Bohemia. In any event, initially, he was able to use his vast resources to recruit and pay for an army of 30,000 men entirely at his own expense. The important point to make here though is that Christian IV was unaware of this developement. He anticipated fighting the Catholic League army under Tilly only – one army, not two. Wallenstein's army – which soon grew to 50,000 and more – changed the balance of military forces quite dramatically. Indeed as 1626 began, the king of Denmark now found himself in a much weaker position. Intervention no longer looked so attractive.

Accordingly, it was decided that Mansfeld would face Wallenstein, Christian of Brunswick would campaign down the Rhine, and the King would take on the Catholic League; however, Mansfeld was defeated at Dessau in April 1626 and although he was able to put together another army and link up with Bethlen Gabor, the plan for joint action had to be abandoned. Mansfeld died in November and Bethlen made yet another peace with the Emperor in December. Christian of Brunswick had died in the previous June thereby ending any possibility of a Rhine campaign. In the meantime, Christian had suffered a decisive defeat at Lutter in August; the fragile unity of the Lower Saxon Circle now collapsed and with the complete failure of the Protestant campaign the way was open for an invasion of Denmark. Early in 1627 Wallenstein (now in full command as Tilly was wounded) marched into Holstein and Jutland (the Danish mainland) before turning East into Mecklenburg and Pomerania and Holstein (see the map on page 39). The Dukes of Mecklenburg had supported Christian IV so the Emperor now deprived them of their titles, transferred their confiscated estates to Wallenstein (February 1627) and the following year made him the sole Duke of Mecklenburg (January 1628). 'If the Emperor could advance his servant, a mere Bohemian nobleman, to the status of prince of the empire and entrust him with the government of an ancient duchy ... he could just as well reduce the princes of the Empire to the status of mere subjects and servants'.[6] Clearly the Emperor had begun to overreach himself.

At the electoral meeting at Mülhausen in October–November 1627, called to discuss the implications of Danish defeat, the Emperor's envoy made it clear that the time had now come to discuss the religious state of Germany and in particular the restoration of

ALBRECHT VON WALLENSTEIN (1583–1634)

-Profile-

Wallenstein was born in Bohemia and given a Protestant upbringing. However, he converted to Catholicism in 1606 and married an elderly, wealthy widow in 1609, which gave him great wealth after her death (1614). During the Bohemian rebellion he remained loyal to Ferdinand and profited enormously from the latter's victory. He was appointed governor of the Kingdom of Bohemia and bought up a large number of confiscated estates so that he came to possess most of north-eastern Bohemia. He eventually assumed the title Duke of Friedland (1623) and in 1625 became generalissimo of the Imperial Army which he raised and paid for at his own expense. He enjoyed considerable military success against the king of Denmark and was elevated to the dukedom of Mecklenburg (1628). His success was resented and at the Electoral Edict of Regensburg his enemies persuaded the Emperor Ferdinand II to dismiss him (August 1630). However, the success of Gustavus Adolphus, king of Sweden, forced the Emperor to recall Wallenstein and he was appointed generalissimo once again in 1632. Although the Imperial general was not victorious at the battle of Lützen in November the death of the Swedish king in that battle created a new political situation. Wallenstein, now no longer indispensable to the Emperor, did not go on the offensive, but sought to conduct negotiations with all and sundry. However, his double dealing and bizarre reliance on astrological predictions undermined his credibility with all parties. By now he had become a liability to the Emperor, who saw him as a traitorous conspirator. Accordingly, in January 1634 he ordered his capture or liquidation and the following month he was assassinated – by an Englishman, an Irishman and a Scotsman! An enigmatic figure, Wallenstein's life became the subject of a dramatic trilogy by the German poet, Schiller.

confiscated Catholic Church lands. However, the campaign of 1628 proved to be something of an anticlimax. The complete defeat of Denmark turned out to be an impossibility: the Danish islands were beyond Wallenstein's reach because he had no fleet. Although the Emperor appointed him 'General of the Oceanic and Baltic Seas' in

February 1628, the Baltic strategy of Olivares (Spain's chief minister from 1622), which envisaged a joint Spanish Imperial fleet with Polish support, never got off the drawing board. Wallenstein attempted to capture the port of Stralsund in the summer of 1628 (May – July), but joint Danish and Swedish action (in itself quite remarkable given their rivalry) thwarted the Imperial commander. Although he defeated Christian again at Wolgast in September, Wallenstein warned the Emperor that if peace were not made Sweden might undertake a full intervention. He also warned that the cost of his army was placing an intolerable burden on the north German states. Clearly the Empire needed peace as much as the Danes and negotiations began in earnest at Lübeck. For these reasons Christian IV got off quite lightly at the peace of Lübeck signed in July 1629. This, however, could not disguise the fact that Denmark had suffered a considerable defeat. The Danish episode was over and once again the Emperor Ferdinand had been triumphant. Indeed the Emperor was at the peak of his power in 1629 but Catholic and Habsburg ascendancy proved to be fragile and short-lived.

3 The Edict of Restitution

> **KEY ISSUE** Why did the Edict alienate everyone and what other reasons led to the collapse of Ferdinand's positon?

Although the Emperor Ferdinand II had expressed his intention to re-Catholicise lost lands at the Electoral meeting at Mülhausen in October 1627, the first draft of the Edict of Restitution was not drawn up until a year later (October 1628) when peace with Denmark was imminent. It was finally issued on 28th March 1629 when a settlement with Christian IV was certain. It stated

1   We, Ferdinand, by the grace of God, Holy Roman Emperor, etc., are determined for the realization both of the religious and profane peace to despatch our Imperial commissioners into the Empire; to reclaim all the archbishoprics, bishoprics, prelacies, monasteries, hospitals and
5   endowments which the Catholics had possessed at the time of the Treaty of Passau [1552] and of which they have been illegally deprived; and to put into all these Catholic foundations duly qualified persons so that each may get his proper due. We herewith declare that the Religious Peace [of 1555] refers only to the Augsburg Confession as it
10   was submitted to our ancestor Emperor Charles V on 25 June 1530; and that all other doctrines and sects, whatever names they may have, not included in the Peace are forbidden and cannot be tolerated. We therefore command to all and everybody under punishment of the religious and the land ban that they shall at once cease opposing our

15 ordinance and carry it out in their lands and territories and also assist
our commissioners. Such as hold the archbishoprics and bishoprics,
prelacies, monasteries, hospitals, etc., shall forthwith return them to
our Imperial commissioners with all their appurtenances. Should they
not carry out this behest they will not only expose themselves to the
20 Imperial ban and to the immediate loss of all their privileges and rights
without any further sentence or condemnation, but to the inevitable
real execution of that order and be distrained by force.[7]

So, under the Edict all land secularised illegally since 1552 was to
return to the Church (this applied particularly to the great Prince
Bishoprics of northern Germany) and Tilly's army was to enforce the
decisions of the commissioners (although as it turned out,
Maximilian would not allow it to do so). In many ways it was the logical climax of the growing antagonism between Protestantism and
Catholicism all over Europe; however, it turned out to be a political
miscalculation of gigantic proportions and caused outrage among
Catholic as well as Protestant princes. Why?

i) For one thing it smacked of Imperial absolutism. It was issued as an
Imperial decree without reference to the Reichstag.[8] It proposed substantial changes and a redistribution of temporal power which would
have considerably strengthened Habsburg power in Europe. In
addition the German princes were reminded that they were not
allowed to make alliances with foreign states. It was high-handed and
arbitrary, and appeared to be as much political as religious in motivation. Coming after the electoral transfer, the deposition of the
Elector Palatine and the Dukes of Mecklenburg and the growth of
Wallenstein's army, the Edict seemed part of a piece: it seemed to
herald an enormous growth in Imperial power.

ii) However, if Ferdinand's attempts to reclaim powers not exercised
since the time of Charles V were disquieting enough, the implications
for the Protestant princes were even more alarming. In particular, it
was feared that many would have to tolerate Catholic enclaves within
their territories or indeed in some cases territories would have to be
broken up altogether. What Ferdinand failed to appreciate though
was that much of his success in the 1620s had been made possible by
the neutrality or even at times active support of the Protestant
princes. Now they were all alienated.

iii) In addition, the assumption upon which the Edict was based – that
the Emperor could rely on the full support of all of Catholic Europe –
had suddenly become invalid. The Emperor could no longer rely on
the support of the Papacy, Spain or France. Urban VIII, Pope since
1623, was not sympathetic to the Habsburg cause and in particular
resented Spanish Habsburg influence in his native Italy. He no longer
subsidised the Emperor and the Catholic League and could not be
relied upon for any active support whatsoever. Ferdinand could no
longer rely on Spain either. From 1627 the war with the Dutch went

badly for Spanish forces and Olivares' involvement in the Mantuan War of Succession (1628–31) in northern Italy proved to be a costly error. Of greatest significance for the future though was the change in French foreign policy. There is an interesting contrast between the Edict of Restitution and Richelieu's Grace of Alès, which brought the French Wars of Religion to an end. Both were signed in 1629, but whereas the Emperor seemed to exacerbate religious tension, Cardinal Richelieu chose to end the conflict with the Huguenots (French Protestants) by compromise and toleration which successfully defused the conflict. Indeed the ending of the religious wars in France meant that the French monarchy could at last embark upon a coherent foreign policy for the first time since the outbreak of the wars in the 1560s. And that foreign policy was to be based not on religous considerations but on reasons of state, that is to say, what is best for the state. Moreover, Richelieu determined that French interests were best served by adopting an anti-Habsburg stance.

iv) However, what was of immediate concern to all the princes was the enormous power wielded by Wallenstein whose army now exceeded 100,000, and whose exactions for its support arbitrarily penalised Catholic and Protestant alike. Indeed, in particular Wallenstein had alienated Maximilian of Bavaria so that the Emperor could no longer rely on the support of the Catholic League either. It was feared that Wallenstein would be the arm of the newly extended Imperial authority. Accordingly in December 1629 at a meeting of the Catholic League, the Elector of Mainz called for his dismissal. In March 1630 he summoned the Electors to meet at Regensburg in June to resolve the matter, and this extract fully reflects the disquiet Wallenstein had generated:

1 The electors, in a dignified and reasonable address, expressed their firm conviction that the whole blame for the misery, disgrace, and infamy, the cruel and unnecessary military exactions, which were daily increasing, rested with the new duke in Mecklenburg [Wallenstein], who, as com-
5 mander of the Imperial forces, had been invested, without the consent of the estates, with such powers as no one before him had ever exercised. The soldiery, now become unspeakably numerous, served no other purpose than to lay waste the common fatherland. Moreover war has been waged upon those against whom it had never been declared. Contributions
10 which, according to the decrees of the diet, no one had the right to demand without the consent of the assembled estates, were levied at the duke's own will and pleasure and wrung from the people in barbarous ways.

The princes went on to make a formal request for Wallenstein's dismissal on July 16th 1630 and surprisingly Ferdinand agreed to comply: the general was dismissed on 13th August. Equally surprising was the fact that Wallenstein also complied. Indeed it would appear that he had come to feel that the maintenance of such a large army was becoming an impossibility. He greeted the end of the responsibility as something of a relief. But why did Ferdinand agree? After all it deprived him of his power to enforce the edict. Tilly took over about a quarter of the Imperial army but he did not have the money to sustain even that small proportion. Ferdinand's military power suddenly evaporated.

There is some suggestion that Ferdinand had already come to distrust Wallenstein but what is certainly true is that his compliance with the Electors' wishes showed that in reality he had no plans to transform the Empire into an absolute monarchy. What is more likely is that he must have thought that by complying he could finally achieve a lasting peace. He went into the meeting hoping to get support for his intervention in northern Italy (Mantua) on behalf of his Spanish cousins as well as support for future assistance to them against the Dutch. He also wished to obtain the election of his son as king of the Romans (in effect heir to the Imperial title). However, in return for his concessions (including a promise that 'no new war will be declared other than by the advice of the Electors'),[9] Ferdinand gained virtually nothing. There was no support for his son becoming king of the Romans and no support for aid to Spain. Although the Edict of Restitution remained intact, Ferdinand had dismissed his general, deprived himself of military power, abandoned the Spaniards in Mantua and yet continued to alienate the Protestants. All in all it was not a very satisfactory outcome.

4 Conclusion

So what we see occur between 1629 and 1630 is a remarkable transformation, from the apogee of Habsburg power to what can only be described as a power vacuum. It would appear that by dismissing his general, Ferdinand had deprived himself of all his political and military power. Of course this might not have mattered had the peace of 1629 lasted, but it did not. Into the vacuum stepped Gustavus Adolphus, king of Sweden.

Whereas the first phase of the war had been about the Habsburg hereditary territories, the second phase raised the prospect of Imperial absolutism, Imperial expansion and a concerted attack on Protestantism. Indeed it was the fear that the Habsburgs generated – that they were going to dominate Europe – that so disconcerted both Sweden and France, and it was to be these two powers that would now prolong the war. Although it remained a German war geographically, more and more decisions would come to be taken elsewhere. Once again the Emperor had been too successful for his own good, but on this occasion he threw away what chance he had of sustaining this success.

References

1 The Elector of Palatinate's territories consisted of two distinct areas: the Rhine or Lower Palatinate, with its capital Heidelberg, and the Upper Palatinate adjacent to both Bavaria and Bohemia – see the map on page 39.
2 Frederick had links to the Dutch (his mother was a princess of Orange),

Brandenburg (his sister was married to the Elector), Sweden via his Aunt and England via his wife. For a family tree see Geoffrey Parker (ed.), *The Thirty Years' War* (Routledge, 1984), pp. 53–4.

3   See Graham Darby, *Spain in the Seventeenth Century* (Longman, 1994), pp. 31–33.

4   For a full discussion of the Spanish match and its consequences see Roger Lockyer, *Buckingham* (Longman, 1981), Chapters 5 and 6.

5   See E. Ladewig Petersen in Parker, as above, p. 72.

6   Ronald Asch, *The Thirty Years' War* (Macmillan, 1997), p. 91.

7   Taken from Gerhard Benecke, *Germany in the Thirty Years' War* (Arnold, 1978), p. 14.

8   Ferdinand in fact did not call an Imperial Diet throughout his reign, relying instead on smaller Electoral Diets and Imperial Decrees. In fact no Imperial Diet met between 1613 and 1640.

9   Quoted by Bodo Nischan in Parker, p. 112.

Summary Diagram
The Habsburgs Triumphant

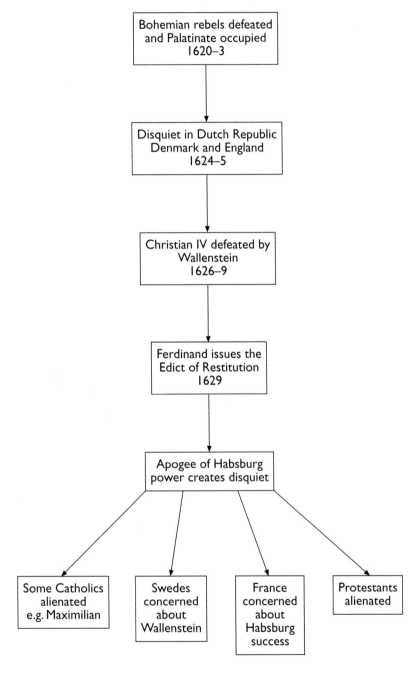

Answering structured questions on Chapter 3

a) Explain why the Bohemian rebels failed. (*4 marks*)
b) Why did the war not end in 1623? (*6 marks*)
c) Why was the Emperor so successful between 1618 and 1629? (*10 marks*)

Hints and Advice

With structured questions you must be careful to tailor the length of your answer to the marks available. It is a common mistake for students to write at length for a question that is worth, say, 4 marks and then to write less for one which is worth 10. Writing at length in answer to the early low mark questions also leaves you little time to complete the entire exercise.

When a question offers 4 marks or 6 marks that does not usually mean that the examiners are looking for four or six points; sometimes they are looking for two or three points and you obtain the extra marks by developing your answer. Thus in the case of a) your two points might be the Bohemians' failure to obtain outside aid and the Emperor's success in doing so. To develop these two points you might refer to the neutrality of the Protestants and the active intervention of the Spanish. As far as b) is concerned your three points might be Ferdinand's success and the disquiet it engendered among the Dutch and the Danes (or indeed the English). To double your marks you would need to develop each point by explaining the change in the balance of power, the obligations the Dutch and English felt towards Frederick, and Danish concerns about the Lower Saxon Circle. Admittedly in question c) you will be required to repeat the points made in a) but you will then need to go on to explain the Emperor's success against the Danes by not only referring to the success of Tilly and Wallenstein's campaigns, but by referring to the failure of the other powers – England, the Dutch, the Swedes and the French – to coordinate any form of viable opposition.

Another type of structured question makes use of alternatives:

1. During the period 1618 to 1629, the course of the Thirty Years' War was affected by: **i)** the policies of the Habsburgs; **ii)** Protestant rebellion; **iii)** the ambitions of the German princes; **iv)** mercenaries.
  a) Explain how any two of these factors particularly affect the development of the War during this period.
  b) Compare the importance of at least three of these factors in the development of the Thirty Years' War from 1618 to 1629.

These two questions are equally weighted.

Source-based questions on Chapter 3

Read the extracts on the Letter of Majesty on page 27, the Defenestration of Prague on page 31 and on the Revised Constitution of Bohemia on page 40, and answer the following questions:

a) According to the Letter of Majesty what religious concessions were made? (*4 marks*)

b) Explain why feelings were running so high in Prague in May 1618 as recorded in the defenestration extract. (*6 marks*)

c) Compare the value of the defenestration extract and the Revised Constituion as sources of evidence for the historian of the Thirty Years' War. (*7 marks*)

d) To what extent do these three sources support the view that the Bohemian War was essentially a political conflict? (*8 marks*)

Hints and Advice

Documentary exercises at AS and A level usually test your understanding of extracts from contemporary sources and/or historians. The objective in a series of questions is usually to test recall (i.e. memory/knowledge), comprehension (your understanding of a source), and comparison and evaluation (how reliable or useful sources are in themselves or in relation to each other). An overall assessment would usually require you to combine an evaluation of all the sources with your knowledge, in answer to a specific question.

Although question a) is comprehension you will need to identify four different concessions for four marks and make sense of the slightly antiquated English translation which might be difficult. Question b) is unusual in that it really requires you to use your knowledge to explain why the defenestration occurred – there is little requirement to discuss the actual document in this question. Question c) is essentially about the nature of the documents as much as their content. Question d) requires reference to the documents but also requires you to have a broader knowledge. This is a difficult question to answer because religion and politics were so inextricably intertwined in those days.

4 Swedish Intervention 1630–35

POINTS TO CONSIDER

This chapter looks at the astonishingly rapid success of Gustavus Adolphus and the almost equally rapid deterioration of the Swedish position after his death. You should consider how Swedish intervention both prolonged the war and yet made the Emperor more realistic in his search for peace.

KEY DATES

1587		Sigismund Vasa becomes king of Poland
1592		Sigsimund becomes king of Sweden
1600		Sigismund formally deposed; war between Sweden and Poland begins
1604		Charles IX becomes king of Sweden
1611		Gustavus Adolphus succeeds as king of Sweden
1626		Swedish conquest of Livonia largely complete
1628		Relief of Stralsund
1629		Truce of Altmark between Sweden and Poland
1630		Gustavus Adolphus lands in Germany
1631	**Sept**	Gustavus wins the Battle of Breitenfeld
1632	**April**	Gustavus defeats Tilly at Rain, Wallenstein recalled
	Nov	Gustavus killed at Lützen
1633		Oxenstierna forms League of Heilbronn
1634	**Feb**	Wallenstein assassinated
	Sept	Swedes defeated at Nördlingen
1635		Peace of Prague

1 Gustavus Adolphus

> **KEY ISSUE** Why did the Swedes intervene and what did they achieve?

a) Background

The reason why the Thirty Years' War did not come to an end with the Peace of Lübeck is because the Swedes intervened. But why did Gustavus Adolphus intervene? Defensive reasons would appear to have been paramount. Although contemporary, as well as later, perception portrayed the Swedish king as the saviour of Protestantism, for him this appears to have been a rather low priority. His motive was altogether more mundane – it was, as we have stated, simply a matter of self-defence. However, Swedish fears had their origins in a disputed succession which went back to the beginning of the century and this did have a religious dimension.

In 1587 Sigismund Vasa, the heir to the Swedish throne and a Catholic, was elected king of Poland, as Sigismund III. When he became King of Sweden in 1592 his faith proved unacceptable to the Protestant Swedish nobility. Accordingly he was formally deposed by his uncle Charles in 1600. Charles became King Charles IX in 1604 and he in turn was succeeded by his son Gustavus Adolphus, in 1611. Thus Gustavus was the son of a usurper and Poland was ruled by his cousin who was the legitimate but Catholic heir. Consequently the rivalry between Sweden and Poland was both dynastic and religious.

This resulted in intermittent warfare that broke out in 1600 and continued into the 1620s with the Swedish conquest of Livonia. Wallenstein's success in northern Germany and Denmark at the same time had thus coalesced with the Polish War into a wider Catholic threat. The possibility of a direct invasion by a Habsburg-Polish alliance seemed very real and for this reason Gustavus had undertaken a joint campaign with erstwhile enemies the Danes in 1628 for the relief of Stralsund (see page 47).

Indeed earlier that same year the Swedish Council gave approval for intervention in Germany in order to counter the Habsburg threat, recognising as Gustavus wrote that 'all the wars which are going on in Europe are linked together and are directed to one end' – i.e. the triumph of the Habsburgs and Catholicism. However, in 1629, as we have seen, the Danes withdrew from the war which deprived the Swedes of an ally. Against this Gustavus was able to arrange, with French mediation, a six year truce – the Truce of Altmark – with the Poles in 1629. This was made by the Polish Diet against King Sigismund III's wishes but it did remove the immediate possibility of a forced Catholic Vasa restoration. However, there was no guarantee that the Habsburg Baltic strategy and the link with the Poles might not be revived in the not too distant future. Hence the decision for intervention was finally made and in the summer of 1630 Gustavus landed on German soil with 16,000 troops. He had no precise plans, no allies and was greeted with suspicion by the Protestant princes. Nevertheless, the dramatic effect of his intervention was to be quite astonishing (all the more so as Sweden was a country with a small population and limited resources) since it brought about a rapid collapse in the Habsburg and Catholic position.

In his famous Declaration of 1630 the Swedish king denounced Wallenstein's aid to the King of Poland in 1629 and the Habsburgs' 'Baltic design'. Little reference was made to German liberties and nothing was said about saving Protestantism. Indeed six years later, the Swedish Chancellor Axel Oxenstierna, referring to 1630, stated the campaign was 'not so much a matter of religion, but rather of saving the *status publicus* [the general political situation], wherein religion is also comprehended'.[1] Nevertheless the religious dimension should not be dismissed altogether; after all, the legitimacy of Gustavus Adolphus' own rule was validated by its link to Protestantism. However, what is clear is that the war had come a long way from being an internal Habsburg dispute, concerned with the 'liberties' of the Bohemian nobility – and indeed some distance from concerns about Frederick V of the Palatinate. It was now a rather different war.

b) The Campaign

Initially Gustavus was cautious; his army was considered to be too small for victory but too large to be fed in the area it occupied, so he took over Eastern Pomerania and Mecklenburg. By securing the German shore against invasion it might be thought that he had fulfilled his main aim, but his initial success was due entirely to a lack of oppositon. There was no enemy to fight! As we have already indicated, the dismissal of Wallenstein and the reduction of the Imperial army had left something of a military vacuum, and had left Gustavus with a dilemma. What was he to do next?

In keeping with his anti-Habsburg strategy Cardinal Richelieu was

GUSTAVUS ADOLPHUS (1594–1632)   *-Profile-*

When Gustavus became king in 1611 at the age of 17, he found his kingdom involved in three wars and in a state of some disarray. However, he quickly conciliated the nobility, created an administrative system and reorganised the army. He made peace with Denmark in 1613, waged a successful war against Muscovy, gaining a part of Finland and Ingria (1617), and fought a long war with Sigismund III Vasa of Poland gaining Livonia (1629) before entering the Thirty Years' War with dramatic consequences.

Known as the 'Lion of the North' he was by all accounts a remarkable individual. He was intelligent – he allegedly spoke seven languages – he was a brilliant general and he possessed that elusive quality, charisma, which earned him the loyalty, respect and affection of those who met him. He had immense self-confidence: the English ambassador wrote – 'he thinks the ship that carries him cannot sink', but later this spilled over into arrogance and overconfidence. His death in battle in 1632 may well have been due to his belief in his own indestructability.

the first to make a treaty with Gustavus and the Treaty of Bärwalde was signed in January 1631. The following terms were agreed:

1 Between Their Most Serene Majesties the Kings of Sweden and France there shall be an alliance for the defence of the friends of each and both of them, for the safeguarding of the Baltic and Oceanic Seas, the liberty of commerce, and the restitution of the oppressed States of the Roman
5 Empire; and also in order to ensure that the fortress and defence-works which have been constructed, in the ports and on the shores of the Baltic and Oceanic Seas, and in the Grisons, be demolished and reduced to the state in which they were immediately before this present German war. And because up to the present the enemy has refused to
10 give a just reparation for the injuries he has caused, and has hitherto rejected all appeals, [the allies] take up arms to vindicate the cause of their common friends. To that end the King of Sweden will at his own expense bring to and maintain in Germany 30,000 foot and 6,000 heavy-armed cavalry. The King of France will contribute 400,000 Imperial
15 *Thaler,* that is, a million *livres tournois,* every year. If God should be pleased to grant successes to the King of Sweden, he is in matter of religion to treat territories occupied by or ceded to him according to the laws and customs of the Empire; and in places where the exercise of the Roman Catholic religion exists, it shall remain undisturbed.

400,000 thalers was not an enormous sum, but it proved to be an important lifeline as the Swedes were desperately short of money as well as other allies. The Protestant princes came together in Leipzig between February and April 1631 to discuss the situation, but were still not prepared to side with the Swedish king.

Meanwhile the Imperial army under Tilly was besieging Magdeburg so in April 1631 Gustavus Adolphus advanced south into Brandenburg. However, he was too late: Magdeburg fell in May and was subject to a massacre which was unusually brutal even by seventeenth-century standards. Up to 20,000 men, women and children died, either killed by Tilly's soldiers or in the flames when the city burnt down. The effect of this on Protestant public opinion throughout Germany was dramatic and instant. The call for revenge reached a crescendo and Protestant pamphleteers looked to the 'Lion from Midnight' (i.e. the north) as he was known, to defend the true faith. This, together with the fact that Swedish troops were on his territory, convinced George William, the Elector of Brandenburg, to side with Gustavus and he signed a treaty in June. After Brandenburg made a deal other Protestant princes followed. Saxony hesitated, but John George joined with the Swedish king in September after Tilly's hungry men had entered Saxony and began plundering.

By this stage Gustavus Adolphus had marched off his maps and was much further south than he had ever intended to go (see the map on page 59). He finally caught up with Tilly at Breitenfeld just north of Leipzig on September 17th. By now he had numerical superiority: to

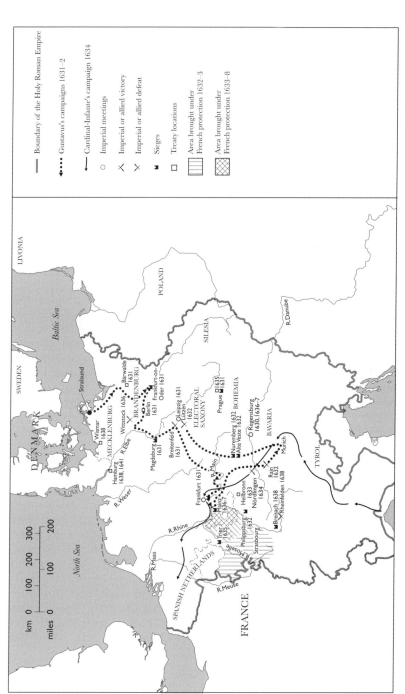

The war in the 1630s

Legend:

Boundary of the Holy Roman Empire

Gustavus's campaigns 1631–2

Cardinal-Infante's campaign 1634

○ Imperial meetings

✕ Imperial or allied victory

✕ Imperial or allied defeat

◼ Sieges

☐ Treaty locations

Area brought under French protection 1632–3

Area brought under French protection 1633–8

his 23,000 soldiers were added 18,000 Saxon troops and they faced an army of 31,000. Breitenfeld proved to be one of the greatest battles of the entire war and a major turning point. Gustavus won a decisive victory; Tilly lost two-thirds of his army, the Catholic position collapsed, and the whole of Germany lay at the Swedish king's feet.

Much to Richelieu's consternation, Gustavus decided to winter in the wealthy Rhineland area (not far from the French border) which could support his ever-growing army. He entered Frankfurt in November and Mainz in December. In the meantime his Saxon allies moved into Bohemia and occupied Prague, also in December. Frederick V, the deposed king of Bohemia and Elector Palatine, joined Gustavus in Mainz in February 1632 but Gustavus was not prepared to restore him until the war was over. Thanks to the resources of many new but largely reluctant allies, the Swedish army was now adequately provisioned and Gustavus Adolphus was for the moment the 'greatest man in Europe'.[2] By Christmas 1631 Swedish armies were in control of half of Germany. There were six armies disposed in an arc from Silesia to the Rhine, garrisoning 100 cities and totalling in excess of 100,000 men.

Gustavus had gone to Germany in search of security but now ruled an empire. His victories inflated his pride and he became increasingly arrogant and contemptuous of the German princes. His success fed his ambitions and he decided to retain Pomerania and it seems he also envisaged a postwar league of Protestant princes under Swedish leadership. But first he had to defeat the Emperor and it seems that a compromise peace would not do. Throughout 1632 he became obsessed with the idea of total victory; he would 'clip the wings of the Imperialists so that they shall not fly again',[3] but it was questionable whether total victory, in a military sense, was really attainable.

In the meantime Tilly, with the remnant of the Imperial army, had gone to Bavaria to recruit a fresh army. In the spring, Gustavus marched south and in April won another victory at Rain where Tilly was mortally wounded. The Swedish king then went on to occupy and plunder Bavaria, and entered Munich, the capital, in May. The Catholic cause now appeared to be in ruins though, at least from the Imperial point of view, this campaign had had the effect of fully committing Maximilian of Bavaria to the Emperor (he had been courted by Richelieu).

Ferdinand II now had little choice but to recall the only commander who seemed capable of saving this situation. Negotiations with Wallenstein began in December 1631 and in April 1632 he was confirmed as commander-in-chief of the Imperial army with what were, in effect, unlimited powers:

1. That the Duke of Friedland [Wallenstein] be not only His Roman Imperial Majesty's, but also the whole Austrian house's and the crown of Spain's generalissimo. ...

4. He should have as security an Imperial pledge on an Austrian hered-
5   itary territory as recompense for his regular expenses.
5. As recompense for his extraordinary expenses, he should be allowed
to exercise the highest jurisdiction in the Empire over the territories
that he occupies.
6. The right to confiscate lands in the Empire shall be his absolutely.
10 7. As in confiscation of lands so also in granting pardons, he, the Duke
of Friedland, shall be allowed to act as he pleases. If anyone should
obtain a safe conduct and pardon from the Imperial court, such shall
have no validity unless it is especially endorsed by the Duke of
Friedland, and it shall apply in good faith and by word of mouth and not
15 in full substance.
8. A genuine pardon is to be only sought from, and granted by, the Duke
of Friedland. For in this matter the Emperor would be too lenient and
allow it to occur that anyone could be pardoned at the Imperial court,
and in this way the means with which to remunerate colonels and offi-
20 cers, as well as looking after the mercenaries as is fit, would be cut off.

His appointment had an immediate effect as Gustavus was forced to
abandon his plans to march down the Danube to Vienna when the
new Imperial commander threatened to cut off his lines of supply.
Accordingly he now set off north in pursuit of Wallenstein.

Aware that another defeat would spell the end for the Imperial
cause, Wallenstein adopted a very cautious strategy. However, he was
able to tie Gustavus down in a fruitless siege around Alte Veste, just
outside Nuremberg for two months while his lieutenants drove the
Saxons out of Bohemia and Silesia.

By the autumn, Gustavus Adolphus's army was suffering serious
desertions and the Swedish king was forced to withdraw; clearly he
was losing the intiative. Wallenstein moved north and occupied
Leipzig, the capital of Saxony, on November 1st. However, at this
point the Imperial commander, believing the campaign season to be
over, began to disperse some of his troops to winter quarters. When
he learnt of this, Gustavus Adolphus decided to march north and give
battle. On November 17th 1632 the two armies finally met at Lützen.
They were in fact quite evenly matched, each with about 20,000 men,
and the battle itself was largely indecisive, though Wallenstein did
withdraw, which technically conceded the field to the Swedes.
However, the most significant outcome of the battle was the death of
Gustavus Adolphus. In the foggy conditions he had been surrounded
and shot three times, in the arm, in the back and in the head. His
corpse was stripped and left unregarded so that for many weeks the
news of his death was not believed. It was a devastating blow to the
Protestant cause, gave new hope to the Catholics and heralded an
altogether more fluid situation. The death of the Swedish king was an
opportunity for peace, but the Emperor saw it as more of an opportunity to recover lost ground.

2 Nördlingen

> **KEY ISSUE** Why did the Swedish position deteriorate?

Gustavus Adolpus was succeeded by his six year old daughter, Christina; consequently the direction of Swedish affairs came under the Chancellor, Axel Oxenstierna. Oxenstierna favoured a settlement whereby Sweden would retain territory in the north, in Pomerania and Prussia, a few outposts further south and secure the south and west by means of a confederation of friendly princes. The latter came into being as the Heilbronn League in April 1633:

> 1 First, the Princes and Estates who have met here with the Crown of
> Sweden under the guidance of the Royal Swedish Chancellor freely
> agree to join together in alliance and give each other mutual aid in order
> that the freedom of Germany and also observance of the statutes and
> 5 laws of the Holy Roman Empire shall once again be observed, and that
> the restitution of the Protestant Estates' rights in matters secular and
> religious shall be kept in a safely concluded peace. Furthermore, the
> Crown of Sweden is to have compensation, and all the separate
> alliances that the Crown of Sweden has made with individual Princes
> 10 and Estates in the four Upper Circles of the Empire shall continue to be
> upheld in all points and not be suspended but rather extended. Such
> separate alliance shall instead enhance the strength of this confedera-
> tion by impressing on every member the importance of and need for
> each and every one's full contributions to be rendered to it.[4]

The League never really fulfilled its purpose and both Saxony and Brandenburg held aloof. The most serious problem that Oxenstierna faced, however, was the mutiny of unpaid soldiery. In order to meet this immediate and widespread danger the Chancellor was forced to give up whole counties and bishoprics to commanders so that they might be compensated. Quite clearly Swedish power was disintegrating but the Imperial Commander-in-Chief did not press home his military and political advantage. Indeed Wallenstein's inactivity in 1633 is something of a puzzle, though he had been granted considerable powers and he spent much of the year in diplomatic negotiation pursuing various peace intiatives and possibly territory and titles for himself. However, his independence, his unreliability and his bizarre behaviour (it was alleged that on arrival in any town he ordered all dogs and cats to be killed because he did not like the noise they made) made him enemies everywhere. At what point and for what precise reasons the Emperor Ferdinand II decided to get rid of his commander-in-chief are not altogether clear, but no doubt the Spanish decision to send an army into Germany and their opposition to Wallenstein's overall command must have been a decisive factor. In any event in February 1634 the Emperor issued a secret order to arrest Wallenstein or kill him if he resisted. Accordingly on the night of February 25th he was brutally murdered by an Englishman, an Irishman and a Scotsman. The absence of any unrest among the Imperial soldiery after this assassination is a measure of how far the generalissimo's stock had fallen.

The Spanish decision to intervene at this juncture was largely due to the collapse of their position in the Spanish Netherlands. The death of the Governor, the Archduchess Isabella, in Brussels in December 1633 made intervention all the more urgent. It was decided to appoint King Philip IV's brother, the Cardinal Infante Ferdinand, as the new governor and send him with a substantial army through Germany. Wallenstein's unhelpful attitude to this project cannot have improved his chances of survival.

The Cardinal Infante set out from Milan in July 1634 and in September he linked up with the new Imperial commander, King Ferdinand of Hungary and Bohemia, the Emperor Ferdinand's son. Together at Nördlingen their joint armies of 33,000 inflicted a decisive defeat on 25,000 Swedes, half of whom were killed. This 'greatest victory of all time', as Olivares put it, cleared the Swedes out of southern Germany and the remnants of the defeated army under Bernard of Saxe-Weimar retreated into Alsace. The way now seemed open for a general settlement.

3 The Peace of Prague

> **KEY ISSUE** Why did the Peace fail to bring the war to an end?

Even before the defeat at Nördlingen many of Sweden's Protestant allies had resented her leadership. John George the Elector of Saxony, in particular, saw himself as the leader of the German Protestants and did not enjoy his subordinate role; he quickly came to terms with the Emperor, signing a preliminary treaty as early as November 1634. Similarly George William, the Elector of Brandenburg, resented Swedish plans to hold on to Pomerania which he considered to be rightfully his; he too was quick to come to terms. For his part the Emperor Ferdinand II was equally eager to end the conflict; he was nearing the end of his life and he needed the two electors' support in order to ensure that his son was recognised as his heir, a matter that was still unresolved. Accordingly he was prepared to make some concessons.

The final treaty was signed on May 30th 1635 in Prague. It was not just between the Emperor and Saxony but for all princes of the Empire who were prepared to accept its terms. The main imperial concession was that the Edict of Restitution was suspended for 40 years, and this represented a significant scaling down of the religious aspect. However, the rest of the terms were rather more favourable to the imperial cause. The 'normative date' for all confessional disputes was set at 1627 – that is to say, the religious situation in that year was to be permanent, was to be frozen in time:

1   Concerning all the ecclesiastical lands and properties that lay within ter-
    ritorial state jurisdiction and that were already secularized before the
    agreement at Passau [of 1552] by the Electors and Imperial Estates who
    are members of the Augsburg Confession, they shall all remain accord-
5   ing to ... the religious peace. However, concerning the ecclesiastical
    lands and properties that were territorial states in their own right and
    were secularized before the agreement at Passau, as well as all those
    ecclesiastical lands and properties that have fallen into the hands of
    members of the Augsburg Confession after the conclusion of the Passau
10 agreement ... those Electors and Imperial Estates who held these lands
    on 12 November 1627 ... shall have complete and free control of the
    same for a period of forty years from the date of this concluded agree-
    ment. And any authority that has been deprived of such lands since 12
    November 1627 shall have them returned without any right to claim
15 costs or damages ...
       In no matters, including those agreed in this treaty and above all
    those concerning the Palatinate affair, shall any armed foreign power be
    tolerated to come onto German soil, unless it is with the ... permission
    of the Emperor.[5]

This date was an acceptable date as it did not threaten the Lutherans of northern and eastern Germany and it enabled the Emperor to retain full control of Bohemia and confirm the transfer of the Electoral title to Maximilian of Bavaria from the Palatinate. Indeed there was nothing in the treaty for Karl Ludwig, the Count Palatine, Frederick's heir, and Calvinism was still not recognised though George William of Brandenburg was a special case – he adhered to the treaty in September. Under some of the other terms of the treaty all the princes were forbidden to enter into foreign alliances, the Catholic League was to be abolished and all armed forces in the Empire now had to swear allegiance to the Emperor (though in prac-tice John George and Maximilian of Bavaria continued to operate fairly independently). Whatever the shortcomings of the Peace of Prague – and there were a considerable number of problems left unresolved – it did defuse the religious tensions and it did point the way towards a lasting settlement. So, why did it fail?

The obvious answer is that it was a wholly German peace – it took no account of the international dimension at all. In particular, it com-pletely ignored the Swedes, whose presence on German soil was still a significant factor. Of course, the reasoning behind this was that most of the signatories to the treaty felt that the Swedes were finished – and they had a point – but it was still necessary to do a deal.

In the aftermath of Nördlingen the government in Stockholm was in something of a panic, brought on particularly by the prospect of renewed warfare with the Poles when the truce expired in 1635. Accordingly many clamoured for peace on any terms or even none at all, though Oxenstierna was made of sterner stuff. Still, Sweden had been abandoned by all her allies, now only possessed a small army under Field Marshal Baner in Pomerania, and faced mutinies from those whose arrears of pay had not been met. Indeed Oxenstierna himself was held hostage for a time in August 1635 by mutinous officers. In addition, Sweden 'was now confronted with a resurgence of German patriotism under the Emperor's leadership, with a universal desire for peace [and] with a fierce hatred of the foreigner'.[6] It is little wonder the regency government made considerable concessions to renew the truce with Poland in September 1635. For his part Oxenstierna set out also in the autumn of 1635 to explore the possibility of peace through the intermediary of Saxony; however, he was subject to humiliation and rebuff. In short, John George told the Swedes to get out and offered them nothing in return. This proved to be a mistaken and short-sighted response and it pushed the Swedes into the arms of the French. However, without French support it is difficult to see how the Swedes could have continued to participate in the war for any length of time.

So, if we had to single out principal reasons why the Peace of Prague failed, it would not just be because it failed to take account of Sweden, but rather because it failed to take account of France as well. Indeed, it was to be France that was mainly responsible for the continuation of the war for another 13 years and it is to France that we turn in the next chapter.

References

1   Quoted in G. Parker, *The Thirty Years' War,* p. 122 and p. 261.
2   M. Roberts, *Gustavus Adolphus,* 2nd edn (Longman, 1992), p. 145.
3   Quoted in Roberts, p. 160.
4   Extract from G. Benecke, *Germany in the Thirty Years' War ,* pp. 14–15.
5   *Ibid.,* pp. 16–17
6   M. Roberts in Parker, p. 158.

Summary Diagram
Swedish Intervention

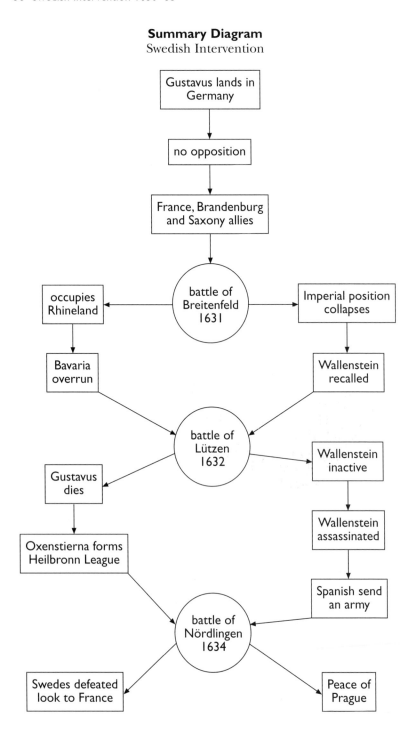

Answering structured and essay questions on Chapter 4

a) What was the dispute between Sweden and Poland? (*4 marks*)
b) Why did Gustavus Adolphus intervene in Germany? (*6 marks*)
c) What impact did Swedish intervention have on the war? (*10 marks*)
d) How do you explain the success of Gustavus Adolphus in the Thirty Years' War?

Source-based questions on Chapter 4

1. 1629–32

Read the extracts from the Edict of Restitution on page 47, from the Electoral Convention on page 49 and from Wallenstein's contract on page 60. Answer the following questions:

a) According to the remarks from the Electoral Convention, what are the main complaints against the new Duke of Mecklenburg? (*4 marks*)
b) Why did the Emperor Ferdinand II issue the Edict of Restitution? (*6 marks*)
c) How useful are the remarks from the Electoral Convention and Wallenstein's contract in helping the historian to assess the importance of the general to the Imperial cause? (*7 marks*)
d) How far do these three extracts explain why the Thirty Years' War did not end with the Edict of Restitution in 1629? (*8 marks*)

2. Swedish Intervention 1630–35

Read the extracts from the Treaty of Bärwalde on page 58, the Confederation of Heilbronn on page 62, and from the Peace of Prague on page 64. Answer the following questions:

a) According to the Peace of Prague, what provisions were made for ecclesiastical lands? (*4 marks*)
b) Explain the references to 'the Palatine affair' (page 64, line 17) and 'any armed foreign power' (page 64, line 17) at the end of the extract from the Peace of Prague. (*6 marks*)
c) Why and in what respects are the terms negotiated by Sweden in the Heilbronn Confederation different from those negotiated in the treaty of Bärwalde? (*7 marks*)
d) How far do these three extracts support the view that the Thirty Years' War could only by ended when the Emperor and German princes combined to expel foreign armies from Germany? (*8 marks*)

5 France Tips the Scales 1635–48

POINTS TO CONSIDER

This chapter will look at the direct intervention of France. Your aim should be to consider whether or not Sweden could have continued the war without French support, whether French aims were realistic, why the war was prolonged, and why peace remained so elusive.

KEY DATES

1629		'Grace of Alais' ends Huguenot revolt
1631		Treaty of Bärwalde
1633		France invades Lorraine
1634		France occupies strongholds in Alsace
1635	May	France declares war on Spain
	Oct	Signs a treaty with Bernard of Saxe-Weimar
1636		Emperor declares war on France
1637		Ferdinand II dies: Ferdinand III succeeds
1638	March	Treaty of Hamburg
	Dec	Capture of Breisach
1639	July	Bernard of Saxe-Weimar dies
1640	May	Catalan revolt
	Sept	Diet of Regensburg
	Dec	Portuguese revolt
1641	June	Treaty of Hamburg renewed
	Jul	Brandenburg–Swedish peace
1642	Nov	2nd Battle of Breitenfeld
	Dec	Richelieu dies
1643	May	Sweden invades Denmark (to 1645)
		Louis XIII dies
		Mazarin first minister;
	Aug	Negotiations begin at Westphalia
1645	March	Battle of Jankov
	Aug	Battle of Allerheim
1646	April	Sweden and Saxony make peace
	Sept	Franco-Imperial preliminary peace
1647	March–Sept	Franco-Bavarian Truce
1648	Jan	Peace of Münster
	May	Battle of Zusmarshausen
	Oct	Swedish siege of Prague and Peace of Westphalia

1 The Tide Turns

KEY ISSUE What were the aims of French foreign policy?

Cardinal Richelieu, Louis XIII's Chief Minister from 1624 to 1642, was determined to revive French prestige and check the power of the Habsburgs, whose territory, he felt, encircled France. 'One's constant aim must be to check the advance of Spain', he wrote.[1] But he was not averse to curbing the Spanish Habsburgs' Austrian cousins as well. Despite being a Cardinal, Richelieu did not seem too concerned with confessional niceties. That is to say, although he was a prince of the Catholic Church, he was not above making a deal with Protestants, if it served French interests – as indeed he did when he brought the Wars of Religion to an end in 1629. After all, his main enemies, the Habsburgs, were Catholics too, so it made sense to make a deal with their Protestant enemies. Thus the Cardinal would appear to have been motivated more by *râison d'état* (reason of state) than by religion, though it was not a phrase he used himself.

For some considerable time, French foreign policy had been disrupted by the Wars of Religion, and it was only after 1629 that a coherent approach to foreign affairs could really be undertaken. As we have seen (page 58) Richelieu sought to curb the Austrian Habsburgs by fighting the Thirty Years' War by proxy – that is to say, by paying others to do the fighting. Accordingly, in 1631 he had made just such a deal with Gustavus Adolphus of Sweden (the Treaty of Bärwalde) and he had subsequently tried to detach Maximilian of Bavaria from the Habsburg cause by signing a Franco-Bavarian treaty in May. However, there was obviously an inherent contradiction in allying with opposing sides in a war; needless to say this policy went badly wrong.

Gustavus Adolphus proved to be no puppet and, as we have seen, actually invaded Bavaria in 1632. Indeed the year 1632 was a traumatic one for Richelieu as his policy appeared to be in tatters. The death of the Swedish king at the end 1632 was not an unwelcome development, though once again it did raise the prospect of a Habsburg revival.

In the meantime, Richelieu had heightened France's control over Lorraine and had begun to secure footholds in Alsace in an attempt to shore up the French frontier (see the map on page 59). In 1634, believing France to be unready for war, he resisted offers of a military alliance with both the Dutch and the Swedes . However, the Habsburg victory at Nördlingen (see page 63) in September transformed the situation and the Cardinal subsequently signed deals with the Dutch in February 1635 and the Swedes in April, though the latter treaty was to come into force only after France had broken with both Spain and the Empire.

CARDINAL RICHELIEU (1585–1642)

Armand Jean Duplessis de Richelieu abandoned a military career to become the Bishop of Luçon at the age of 22. In 1614 he became advisor to Marie de Medici, the regent, and in 1616 Secretary for War. However, with the fall of Marie, he fell too and returned to his diocese. He was instrumental in reconciling Marie with her son Louis XIII in 1621 and was rewarded with a Cardinalate in 1622. In 1624 he became first minister and in a series of campaigns defeated the Huguenots. In 1629 he brought the Wars of Religion to an end by means of toleration. By this time he had fallen out with Marie, who opposed his deal with the Huguenots and his anti-Habsburg foreign policy.

He nearly fell from power in 1630, but the 'Day of the Dupes' proved to be the Queen Mother's downfall. Richelieu was by now firmly established and by means of propaganda and patronage he was able to trumpet his indispensability and fill key positions with his supporters. Although their relationship was often difficult, the dilatory Louis XIII relied entirely on the Cardinal and supported him through a series of conspiracies. Richelieu's contribution to French revival has undoubtedly been exaggerated (not least by himself!), but his ability to remain in office for 18 years was remarkable and gave French policy a continuity that it had lacked for a long time.

In March 1635, the Spanish had carried off the Archbishop Elector of Trier as their prisoner, a deliberately provocative act since the archbishop was nominally under French protection. Richelieu's personal reputation as well as his foreign policy was at stake and accordingly on May 19th 1635 France declared war on Spain – but only Spain. This was in accordance with the Cardinal's view that Philip IV was the main enemy; Richelieu still had no intention of embarking on a war within Germany, though the situation there was quite serious. All that remained of the Heilbronn League was a handful of minor princes, so France agreed to subsidise both William of Hesse-Kassel and his army of 10,000, and Bernard of Saxe-Weimar and his army of 18,000 (October 1635). The Swedes were left to fend largely for themselves. Oxenstierna was reluctant to commit Sweden to a subordinate role to France and accordingly the Treaty of Wismar of March 1636 between the two countries, was left unratified. The Swedish Chancellor seemed to be vindicated when in October 1636 his general, Baner, won a great victory at Wittstock which effectively eliminated Brandenburg from the war. However, this success proved short-lived and by the end of 1637 the Swedes had once again been forced back to the Pomeranian shore. There was little alternative to the French alliance now and in March 1638 Oxenstierna swallowed his pride and ratified the Wismar agreement by means of the Treaty of Hamburg. This bound each side to the other for three years and provided Sweden with much needed subsidies.

1638 was important for another reason, for in that year Bernard of Saxe-Weimar won the battle of Rheinfelden in March and took Breisach in Alsace in December thereby gaining the upper hand in the Rhineland area. Fortunately for the French Bernard died without an heir the following year; this was fortunate because France had been committed to the formation of a new ducal territory under Bernard in Alsace. Now Richelieu not only 'inherited' his territory, but was able to take over his army as well, thereby directly controlling the Rhineland campaigns. The Cardinal, it seems, had a large amount of luck in this matter.

Although Richelieu had sought to concentrate on Spain and avoid a direct clash with the Emperor, Ferdinand II had himself declared war on France in March 1636. He died the following year but not before ensuring that he would be succeeded by his son, Ferdinand III. Given the deterioration of the Habsburg position over the next few years the new Emperor proposed that a full Imperial Diet should meet for the first time since 1613, to consider a general peace. It convened in September 1640. Here the Emperor was forced to make considerable concessions, abandoning the Edict of Restitution and allowing princes other than Electors to send envoys to negotiate with France and Sweden.

The previous year Baner had defeated the Saxons at Chemnitz and although a joint operation with the Rhineland army in 1640 achieved little, the French conquest of Artois in the Spanish Netherlands and the revolts in Catalonia and Portugal ensured that Spanish aid would no longer be available to assist Vienna. The tide was turning. In 1641 Baner even shelled Regensburg where the Diet was meeting.

In that year also Brandenburg abandoned the Emperor and reached a ceasefire with the Swedes. Baner died, the Swedish army mutinied and Oxenstierna was left with little alternative but to renew the Treaty of Hamburg. However, what was really significant about the renewal of the treaty was the fact that France and Sweden now agreed to remain allied for an unlimited period of time – in fact, until the war ended and a satisfactory peace had been concluded. This clearly prolonged the war. Now the Swedes were prepared to fully support French policy in Germany in return for cash. Without French money their continuing campaign was simply not viable. Indeed it was really French money that tipped the scales, financing the Swedes in northern Germany and directly controlling the army of the Rhineland. Without French money it is hard to see how these armies could have continued to function. And no one could match French expenditure – not the Emperor, not even Spain. For example, total annual Spanish military expenditure in this period was only about half that of France after 1635.[2]

DATE	EXPENDITURE IN MILLIONS OF THALERS
1630	9.2
1631	6.0
1632	7.4
1633	6.7
1634	9.9
1635	16.5
1636	13.5
1637	11.0
1638	12.8
1639	12.8
1640	12.5
1641	13.4
1642	13.0
1643	19.4
1644	19.0
1645	18.0
1646	15.4
1647	15.8
1648	13.0[3]

Table: Overall French Military Expenditure (i.e. all theatres of war)

With Spain on the rack and his allies contemplating separate peace settlements with France and Sweden, Ferdinand III's position was becoming very difficult. Whereas in the past the fortunes of war had oscillated back and forth they now seemed to be going only one way, a fact borne out by the devastating victory won by the new Swedish commander, Torstensson, at Breitenfeld (again) in November 1642 (for this and other battles in the 1640s, see the map on page 73). The Imperial army was decimated and Saxony overrun. The Emperor needed peace; Germany needed peace, but the various parties had different ideas about what was actually going to constitute a satisfactory settlement.

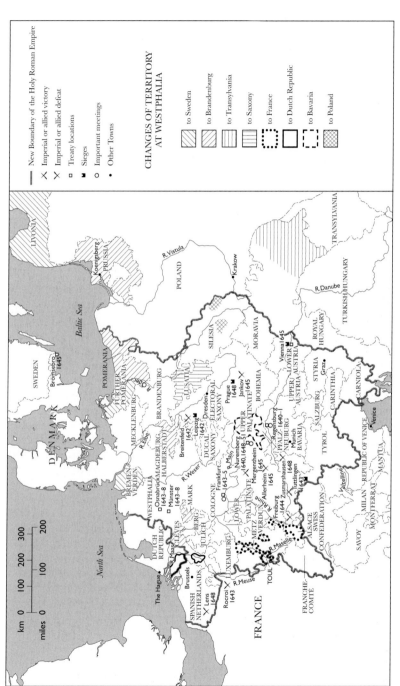

The war in the 1640s and the peace settlement

Legend:

CHANGES OF TERRITORY AT WESTPHALIA

- ⸺ New Boundary of the Holy Roman Empire
- ✕ Imperial or allied victory
- ✕ Imperial or allied defeat
- ☐ Treaty locations
- ◼ Sieges
- ○ Important meetings
- • Other Towns

- to Sweden
- to Brandenburg
- to Transylvania
- to Saxony
- to France
- to Dutch Republic
- to Bavaria
- to Poland

2 The Search for Peace

> **KEY ISSUE** What did Sweden and France want from a peace settlement?

Although the issue of the secularised church lands was solved at Regensburg by the Emperor's abandoment of the Edict of Restitution, the real obstacle to peace in Germany was now the aims and ambitions of Sweden, and, in particular, France. Swedish aims consisted of some form of territorial compensation (security), be it all of Pomerania or just a few bases on the Baltic shore, an amnesty for her few allies, the prevention of the enslavement of the empire, whatever that might mean, and, most importantly, financial compensation for the contentment of the soldiery (i.e. back-pay). In a letter Oxenstierna wrote to his son in 1644, it appears that concern over the state of the Empire was a subordinate aim:

> So long as 'the restoration of affairs of the Empire to their original state' is our pretext for wanting changes in our favour ... we must justify all our doing in the light of the same.[4]

Richelieu, on the other hand, was most concerned about the Empire. He envisaged nothing short of a new framework for European politics which would guarantee a lasting peace and at the same time confirm France's position as pre-eminent among the powers. This would involve a general peace encompassing both branches of the Habsburg Empire, the Spanish and the Austrian. However, with regard to Germany this new framework was hardly compatible with existing imperial institutions as long as the Emperor was a Habsburg, so it would appear that Richelieu envisaged either superceding or replacing the Empire altogether, or at the very least neutralising the role of the Emperor within it. In any event, the positions held by Sweden and particularly France were some distance from anything the Emperor was prepared to consider, even though his situation was deteriorating.

Richelieu's general French pacification was not to be. He died at the end of 1642 quickly followed by his master, Louis XIII, the following year. However, French policy did not change. It came to be controlled by Cardinal Mazarin who gambled on a quick victory and increased French military expenditure by nearly fifty per cent (see the table on page 72). Despite this in 1643 the first diplomatic envoys arrived at Münster and Osnabrück to discuss peace. These two cities had been specified for negotiations by the renewed Treaty of Hamburg between France and Sweden in 1641. France, Spain and the other Catholic participants were based at Münster, Sweden and her allies at Osnabrück. The Swedish delegate, Johan Adler Salvius, summed up the position of France and Sweden:

1 For thirty years no Imperial Diet has been held, and in the interim the emperor has managed to usurp everything by right of sovereignty. This is the high road to absolute rule and the servitude of the territories. The crowns [of Sweden and France] are seeking, as far as they are able,
5 to obstruct this, for their security rests on the liberty of the German territories.[5]

However, the Emperor was able to resist his enemies' demands and delay negotiations because of the outbreak of war between Sweden and Denmark in 1643. Ferdinand had been negotiating with Christian IV for just such an eventuality; however, the Swedes got wind of these talks and determined on a pre-emptive strike. Within a year the Danes were defeated and Christian had to sign a humiliating peace in 1645. Moreover an Imperial army of 18,000 under Count Gallas, despatched to assist the Danes, fell foul of disease, desertion and a lack of supplies, and fell apart without ever coming to battle. This was not the outcome Ferdinand had anticipated, as he had hoped to bring about Swedish defeat. The scene was now set for his own defeat.

3 Habsburg Defeat

> **KEY ISSUE** Why did the Emperor finally agree to serious negotiations?

In 1645 the Swedes decided on an invasion of Bohemia and at Jankov, near Prague, Torstensson inflicted a decisive defeat on the Imperial army which suffered the loss of half its men. The emperor had risked all his resources and staked his reputation on this encounter and it was a blow from which the Imperial army never really recovered. The Emperor himself and his family now fled to Graz. So that he could receive no aid from Bavaria, it was decided to launch an attack there too.

Thus far the French army of the Rhine under Turenne had not been able to get the better of the Bavarian army and had suffered a series of setbacks at Tuttlingen in 1643, Freiburg in 1644 and at Mergentheim in 1645. However, with the arrival of Swedish reinforcements, Turenne was finally able to inflict a decisive defeat on the Bavarians at Allerheim in August 1645, which destroyed Maximilian's army as a viable fighting force. After Jankov and Allerheim, there was no longer a Catholic army to withstand the Swedes and the French. Accordingly, in September John George of Saxony reluctantly signed a ceasefire with the Swedes; shortly afterwards the Emperor issued an amnesty for all his rebellious vassals and at the end of November his chief negotiator, Count von Trauttmannsdorf, arrived at Münster with instructions to negotiate a peace. Thus serious discussion about a settlement finally got under way in 1646 and it looked as though the war might be over. However, many textbooks suggest it took another defeat of the Bavarians at Zusmarshausen in May 1648 and a siege of Prague in the autumn (in which the royal regalia were carried off by the Swedes) to persuade the Emperor and Maximilian that resistance was futile. However, in reality the last year of the war was a little more complicated than that. Increased demands by Mazarin led to the continuing hostilities and the war only really came to an end because of France's inability to carry on, as we shall see in the next chapter. Just as France had prolonged the war, so too France was able to end it, albeit unwillingly.

References

1 Quoted in R.J. Knecht, *Richelieu* (Longman, 1991), p. 84.
2 Graham Darby, *Spain in the Seventeenth Century* (Longman, 1994), pp. 12–13.
3 R.J. Bonney, *The King's Debts* (Oxford UP, 1981), Appendix 2, Table 2.
4 Quoted in Geoffrey Parker, *The Thirty Years' War* (Routledge, 1984), p. 180.
5 Quoted in Parker, pp. 173–4. N.B. the contention that no Diet had been held for thirty years is of course not correct.

Summary Diagram
France Tips the Scales

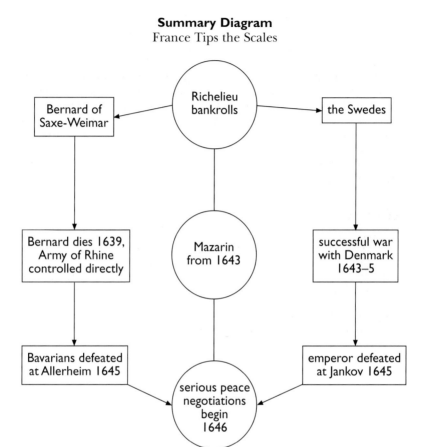

a) What were the aims of Richelieu's foreign policy? (*4 marks*)
b) Why did Richelieu become directly involved in the Thirty Years' War? (*6 marks*)
c) What were the obstacles to peace during this period? (*15 marks*)
d) Why and with what results did France enter the Thirty Years' War?

6 The Peace of Westphalia

POINTS TO CONSIDER

This chapter will take you through the negotiations and terms of the Peace before attempting a summation. You should consider why the peace came about when it did and why it took the form that it did.

KEY DATES

1643		Negotiations begin at Westphalia
1645		Trauttmannsdorf arrives at Westphalia
1646	Jan	Dutch envoys arrive at Münster
	April	Peace between Sweden and Saxony
	Sept	Franco-Imperial preliminary peace
1647	Jan	Spanish-Dutch truce
	March–Sept	Franco-Bavarian truce
1648	Jan	Peace of Münster
	May	Fronde begins
	Aug	Swedish Imperial preliminary peace
	Oct	Peace of Westphalia

1 Negotiations

> **KEY ISSUE** What were the aims of the major participants?

All the Estates and princes of the Holy Roman Empire were invited to participate in the peace, along with the Imperial, French, Swedish, Spanish and Dutch envoys. Consequently there were a grand total of 176 plenipotentiaries representing 196 rulers. This not only put a strain on the negotiations but on the accommodation as well – two to a bed was not uncommon! Because there were so many particpants and so many conflicting interests, it is hard to discern a pattern of negotiation. In any event, the pace and pattern of both negotiations and concessions varied according to the fortunes of war. As one delegate put it: 'in winter we negotiate, in summer we fight'.[1] Still, three phases have been identified:

i) The period from 1643 to the arrival of Count Trauttmannsdorf, Ferdinand's representative, in November 1645, which was largely procedural.

ii) From the Count's arrival to his departure in June 1647, when almost all the disputes in both the Dutch and German conflicts were settled.

iii) The period until October 1648; a final settlement was not reached until this time because Mazarin decided to increase French demands and continued the war until such a time as he could no longer do so.[2]

What were the aims of the major participants? The Emperor clearly wanted a full and final peace settlement as his situation was desperate. As we have already stated, after 1645 he had no army to speak of, the Swedes controlled northern Germany and could enter Bohemia at will and similarly the French controlled the Rhineland and could ravage Bavaria at will. Consequently Ferdinand gave Trauttmannsdorf instructions to make far-reaching concessions, were they to be necessary. Thus in religious matters the status of possessions, property and allegiance could ultimately revert to 1618 if 1627 could not be maintained (the normative date decided at the Peace of Prague); Sweden was to be granted the whole of Pomerania; France was to be given the Habsburg possessions in Alsace (the Sundgau); and Karl Ludwig (Frederick's son) of the Palatinate could be granted an additional (i.e. eighth) electoral title. These concessions were considered to be very much the last resort, but they do indicate the Emperor's firm desire for a settlement.

Mazarin wanted a universal peace encompassing both Spain and the Emperor. However, negotiations with Spain collapsed in 1646. In that year Philip IV's son and heir, Baltazar Carlos, died and this precluded the proposed marriage alliance involving his daughter, Maria Teresa, with Louis XIV. In any event, the French also wanted substantial territorial concessions from the Spanish which Philip IV was not willing to grant. Spain preferred to do a deal with the Dutch (achieved in January 1647, ratified at Münster in January 1648) and keep fighting. The best Mazarin could hope for was a deal with the emperor and subsequently his aim came to be to create a rift between Madrid and Vienna. As far as Germany was concerned French instructions had been drawn up in 1643 and were largely the work of Richelieu. France wanted to destroy the Emperor's influence by strengthening the autonomy (i.e. independence) of the individual princes and by replacing the existing Imperial institutions by a French-led Federation. However, these plans were unpopular with the German princes, who valued the Holy Roman Empire and preferred a circumscribed (i.e. limited in authority) Emperor to dominance by France and Sweden. Trauttsmannsdorf had little difficulty in resisting those demands. French territorial demands (most of Alsace and parts of Lorraine) were quite modest because France mainly wanted Spanish territory. Mazarin was able to obtain Alsace in return for 1.2 million thalers in a deal with the Emperor in September 1646.

Sweden's aims remained fairly constant (see page 74), though greater emphasis was placed on the reduction of imperial power and increased territorial demands as the military situation improved: Sweden now demanded all of Pomerania, parts of Mecklenburg, the

CARDINAL MAZARIN (1602–61)

-Profile-

Jules Mazarin was born Guilio Mazarini in Italy and began his career in the diplomatic service of the Pope. He was papal nuncio to France from 1634 to 1636 and subsequently entered French service and became a naturalised Frenchman (1639). Two years later he became a cardinal through the influence of Richelieu, who before his death recommended Mazarin to the the king. He became first minister in 1643 after the king's death and he owed his position to the close relationship he enjoyed with the regent, Anne of Austria. He increased taxation in order to win the wars against the Habsburgs but this led to the collapse of governmental authority and civil disorder known as the Fronde which forced him to abandon the war in Germany. He was lucky to survive but owed his position to the devotion of Anne, the support of the young Louis XIV and the disunity of the opposition. He was eventually able to gain the upper hand against the Spanish by allying with Oliver Cromwell, and the Treaty of the Pyrenees was signed in 1659. This brought the war to a successful conclusion and led to the the marriage of Maria Teresa and Louis XIV in 1660. Mazarin died the following year leaving an immense fortune. One of his important legacies was the political education he gave to Louis XIV.

bishoprics of Bremen and Verden, and a huge indemnity of 30 million thalers (c. 6 million pounds). Needless to say these demands created enormous opposition as one of their negotiators, Johan Salvius, recognised in a letter to Queen Christina written in 1646:

> People are beginning to see the power of Sweden as dangerous to the 'balance of power'. Their first rule of politics is that the security of all depends on the equilibrium of individuals. When one begins to become powerful ... the others place themselves, through unions or alliances,
> 5 into the opposite balance in order to maintain the equipoise.[3]

Sweden had absolutely no legitimate claim to Pomerania whatsoever; it belonged by rightful inheritance to Frederick William, the Elector of Brandenburg, who was tenacious in support of his rights – so much so that he was able to enlist the support of Mazarin who did not want to see the Swedes become too powerful. Accordingly, the Cardinal decided to build up Brandenburg as a counterweight to Swedish power and in February 1647 the Swedish envoys were persuaded to agree to a partition of Pomerania. This incident illustrates the tension between the erstwhile allies, a tension Trauttmannsdorf was able to exploit in other ways too. For instance, the Swedes demanded religious toleration within the Habsburg lands, for the Bohemians in particular. The Emperor was able to resist this demand quite firmly in the knowledge that the French had little sympathy for Bohemian Protestants, and would not support Sweden on this issue. It is interesting to reflect that the group of people who had been instrumental in starting the conflict could so easily be swept aside at the peace settlement. The Swedish envoys were not only prepared to give in over the Bohemian Protestants and Pomeranian partition, but were also prepared to settle for an indemnity of 5 million thalers, a fraction of their original demand. Sweden's willingness to compromise was the result of the pressure being placed on the negotiatiors by Queen Christina who was now eager for a quick settlement. In 1647 she wrote:

> 1 I desire above all things a safe and honourable peace. And since the question of our indemnity has already been disposed of, and only matters still to be arranged are the contentment of the soldiery and the grievances of the States of the Empire, it is my will that you ... will
> 5 without delay bring the negotiation to a satisfactory conclusion: for the [German] States, and in the matter of our indemnity and the contentment of the soldiery, you will obtain the best terms that are to be had without risk of a rupture; and you will refrain from protracting the negotiation, as you have done in the past.

As far as religion was concerned, matters of territory and allegiance had been addressed in the Peace of Prague and at Regensburg but the status of Calvinism and the normative date still had to be resolved. As we have already indicated (see page 74) the delegates divided up along confessional lines; however, even within the same denomination there was no agreement. Among the Catholics there were those who were prepared to make varying degrees of compromise, while on the other hand there were those who were adamant that they did not want to make any. Similarly, the Protestants were divided between Lutherans and Calvinists. However, overall the Protestants proved to be more united and that is why the final agreement on religious issues reached in March 1648 was favourable to them.

Agreement was postponed because Mazarin decided to increase French demands. Unnerved by Spain's deal with the Dutch (which he had tried to sabotage) the Cardinal demanded the Emperor's neutrality in the ongoing conflict; he also sought for Louis XIV status as a prince of the Empire, an indemnity, and the restoration of the whole of the Palatinate to Karl Ludwig. This caused the war to be rekindled (see page 76), though with the onset of civil unrest in

France in the summer of 1648 (the Fronde), Mazarin reluctantly changed his tune and by August was convinced of 'our need to make peace at the earliest opportunity'. Consequently he dropped his extra demands and agreed to a settlement (though the Emperor did agree not to aid his Spanish cousin).

Ultimately the treaties were signed by the Imperial plenipotentiaries, a select number of delegates from the Empire and the foreign powers. Any number of other members of the empire could sign but whether or not they did so, the peace still applied to them.

2 Terms

KEY ISSUE What were the principal clauses of the Treaty?

The Peace of Westphalia was signed simultaneously at Münster and Osnabrück on 24th October 1648 and consisted of 128 clauses. The main parts may be summarised as follows:

1   The principle of *cuius regio, eius religio* (i.e. whoever owned the territory could determine the religion) was reaffirmed, but construed to relate only to public life, so that attendance at the established church was no longer compulsory and freedom of private worship was permitted. Moreover, any subsequent change of religion by the ruler was not to affect that of his subjects.

2   Calvinism was recognised within the Confession of Augsburg and was thus protected by the Augsburg settlement of 1555. The Edict of Restitution, shelved in 1635, was abandoned, and except within the Bavarian and Austrian lands (including Bohemia) the retention of all land secularised before 1624 was allowed.

3   In matters of religion there were to be no majority decisions taken by the Diet. Instead both sides were to meet separately to prepare their cases and disputes were to be settled only by compromise.

4   To all intents and purposes the separate states of the Holy Roman Empire were recognised as sovereign members of the Diet, free to control their own affairs independently of each other and of the emperor. Article 63 states:

i   They shall enjoy without contradiction the right of suffrage in all deliberations concerning the affairs of the empire, especially when the business in hand touches the making or interpreting of law, the declaring of war, levying of taxes, raising or maintenance of troops, the erection on

5   imperial behalf of new fortresses or the garrisoning of old in the territories of the states, also the conclusion of peace or of alliances, or similar matters. In these and like concerns nothing is in future to be done or admitted except by the common free choice and consent of the imperial states. But particularly the individual states shall be for ever at

10 liberty to enjoy the right of making alliances with each other and with
other parties for their own support and security; always provided that
such alliances shall not be directed against the emperor or empire, nor
against the public peace of the empire, nor above all against the present
treaty; and in everything without prejudice to the oath which everyone
15 is bound to take to emperor and empire . . .[4]

5 Maximilian retained his electoral title and the Upper Palatinate.
6 A new electoral title was created for Karl Ludwig, the son of the
former Elector Palatine, on his restoration to the Lower Palatinate.
7 John George of Saxony was confirmed in his acquistition of Lusatia.
8 The terms of the Treaty of Xanten (1614), assigning Cleves, Mark
and Ravensburg to the elector of Brandenburg, were confirmed.
In addition, Frederick William acquired Cammin, Minden and
Halberstadt, along with the succession to Magdeburg.
9 The emperor's claim to hereditary rights in Bohemia, Moravia and
Silesia was established. The Sundgau was surrendered to France.
10 Sweden had acquired her mainland provinces of Jemteland,
Herjedalen and Halland, with the islands of Gotland and Osel by
the Treaty of Brömsebro (1645). The Peace of Westphalia confirmed her control of the river-mouths of the Oder, the Elbe and
Weser – virtually the entire German coastline – by the occupation
of western Pomerania, Stettin, Stralsund, Wismar, the dioceses of
Bremen and Verden and the islands of Rügen, Usedom and
Wollin. She was paid an indemnity of 5 million thalers.
11 France acquired the Sundgau and, in effect, Lower Alsace, though the
six free cities along with the city and bishopric of Strassburg retained
their membership of the Diet. In Lorraine, her occupation of the
bishoprics of Metz, Toul and Verdun (Treaty of Câteau-Cambrésis
1559) was confirmed, along with her more recent gains of Moyenvic,
Baccarat and Rambervillers. Other acquisitions inclued Pinerolo in
Savoy, and Breisach and Philippsburg on the right bank of the Rhine.
12 The United Provinces were declared independent of Spain and
also of the Holy Roman Empire (Switzerland was also no longer
part of the Empire).
13 No prince of the empire, not even the Emperor, could ally with
the Spanish Monarchy.

3 Assessment

> **KEY ISSUE** Who gained and who lost from the Peace?

An overall assessment is not easy to make. By and large the treaties
defused those problems which had helped cause the war. Although
confessional loyalties remained important, the age of religious wars
was over in Germany. The religious settlement proved to be realistic

and lasting, though the Pope, Innocent X, was unambiguous in his condemnation:

1   Consumed by zeal for the house of the Lord, we are especially con-
    cerned with the endeavour everywhere to maintain the integrity of the
    orthodox faith and the authority of the Catholic Church, so that the
    ecclesiastical rights of which we have been appointed guardian by our
5   Saviour shall not in any way be impaired by those who seek their own
    interest rather than God's, and that we may not be accused of negli-
    gence when we shall render account to the Sovereign Judge.
    Accordingly it is not without deep pain that we have learned that by
    several articles in the peace concluded at Osnabruck and at Munster in
10 Westphalia, great prejudice has been done to the Catholic religion. By
    various articles in one of these treaties of peace the ecclesiastical pos-
    sessions which the heretics formerly seized are abandoned to them and
    to their successors, and the heretics, called those of the Augsburg
    Confession, are permitted the free exercise of their heresy in various
15 districts.[5]

This condemnation had been anticipated by the signatories and was expressly rejected by them – even by Catholics. To some extent Innocent X's predecessor, Urban VIII, must bear some responsibility for this since his anti-Habsburg stance did much to undermine Catholic unanimity (though not as much as Richelieu). Whether or not this was the last religious war, and whether or not religion ceased to be so important after this war, are moot points and are considered in the next chapter (see pages 90–93).

As far as the political settlement is concerned, the Peace was remarkably conservative and legalistic. It was seen more as a restatement of old rights rather than anything new. That is to say much that had been *de facto* (i.e. a matter of fact or common practice) was now *de iure* (legal) – such as the autonomy of the princes. Of course that is not to say there were no innovations – the creation of an eighth electorate was just such a thing – but established custom and legal rights were usually to be preferred.

Within the Empire, Saxony, Bavaria and Brandenburg had all grown in size and importance. The tendency here was towards full sovereign independent states. Indeed the Elector of Brandenburg did well from the treaty out of all proportion to his participation because, as we have already indicated, Mazarin favoured his cause (see page 80). However, these larger states were still not a match for the Emperor who, among other things, retained the prestige of precedence. Ferdinand III had undoubtedly lost power – for instance, he lost the right to levy taxes and declare war without the consent of the Diet – but he remained the foremost prince in Germany. Moreover, many of the smaller states were too small to exploit the rights and liberties they had been granted. An independent foreign policy and an alliance with a foreign power were quite simply unrealistic and impractical options for many smaller imperial states. Thus the autonomy of the princes remained limited. They preferred the security of the Holy Roman Empire; they relied on the Emperor and were happy to seek his protection – particularly now he was not seen as a predator. Fear that the Habsburgs might subordinate the Empire to greater central control had encouraged their enemies to intervene – but whether or not this was a realistic fear is a moot point. Certainly after 1648 the Imperial bureaucracy became more cumbersome and made Habsburg control less practical; however, recent research is beginning to question the idea that Westphalia fixed the Empire's constitution in its final form. It is now thought to have been more receptive to change. Moreover, under Ferdinand's successor, Leopold (1658–1705), the Emperor's prestige underwent a considerable revival after his success against the Turks in the 1680s. In fact Imperial policy continued to be decided by the Emperor.

The Emperor himself was now very much strengthened within his hereditary territories: both religious and political opposition in Bohemia and Austria had been crushed, the hereditary lands were now ruled as a single unit, and interference from imperial institutions was largely excluded after 1635. Accordingly, the Emperor was in a far better position than he had been in 1618. Of course compared with the dizzy heights of 1629 there had been reverses – Ferdinand III had undoubtedly lost the last part of the war – but he was able to retain some of his father's early successes and, given his dire military situation at the end, the final settlement was not unfavourable to him. So, the Emperor did not do too badly and, as we have indicated, there still existed a reservoir of considerable goodwill towards him among the princes. There was of course something of 'better the devil you know' in this, as the alternative, Franco-Swedish dominance, was not an attractive one. For this reason Franco-Swedish ambitions to restructure or replace the Empire were never realistic options. The Princes resisted Franco-Swedish attempts to destroy the Imperial constitution and that is why the Emperor got off lightly.

Indeed a good case can be made for suggesting that French foreign policy in the Thirty Years' War was largely a failure. Mazarin failed to get his universal peace; he failed to transform the Empire; he failed to reduce the power of the Emperor significantly and he failed to increase French influence in Germany by very much. All the money and effort expended had in fact brought France very little in return. Some historians gloss over this by the suggestion that Mazarin laid the foundations for future success by obtaining territory with ill-defined jurisdictions over adjacent lands; however, this just seems to be a way of trying to make the most of the paltry amount of territory France actually obtained. It is also to make the mistake of reading history backwards since it cannot be stated categorically that in 1648 these jurisdictions would be exploited in the future. And although it could be argued that France obtained this territory without membership of the Imperial Diet so as not to recognise the overlordship of the Emperor, equally it could be argued that the Emperor was successful in keeping France out of the Empire.

Some historians also argue that another 'achievement' of Mazarin was to exclude Spain from the Treaty. But this is plainly erroneous, since Spain did not want to be part of the treaty in the first place. Of course getting the Emperor to agree to withold support from Madrid might be considered an achievement, but Ferdinand was in no position to give much help anyway. That Mazarin himself saw the peace as unsatisfactory can be appreciated from this letter he wrote to the French envoy, Servien, in October 1648:

1 It might perhaps have been more useful for achieving a general peace if the war could have been pursued a little longer in Germany, instead of our haste to find an accommodation as we have now done. Yet this would have implied that we were in a position to prolong negotiations
5 when instead there was the threat that Sweden might have betrayed us and acted on her own urgent desire to conclude hostilities. The fear of such an unpleasant event overrode all other considerations. I think that the fear of total collapse by the emperor which, considering his pathetic situation, was unavoidably imminent, may have been enough to invite
10 sympathy from the Spaniards, cause them somewhat to soften their harsh stand and protect him from such a blow. Whereas now they consider him to be secured by the conclusion of peace, despite the conditions, which are quite harsh to him, and they take no more notice of him, nor do they seem to worry about his position, which may other-
15 wise have been a more serious reason for bringing them to conclude peace. We can be quite sure that the greatest aid to the emperor has now come from us in that we forced him into making peace, for otherwise his total ruin would have been inevitable.

Furthermore, I gather from a reliable source that the Emperor –
20 whether to soften the blow of leaving the Spaniards, to which he is now committed, or whether he really intends to make use of it, as he has let it be known – has assured the king of Spain through the archduke that all that he has done has only occurred in order to deflect the full force of destruction that almost threatened to engulf him, and that this peace
25 is certainly damaging in its hard terms, but that given the situation under which it was concluded, it is very advantageous. A great number of fortified places and lands have been returned to him, which he has already lost, giving him the opportunity to save the rest, which under the circumstances would have been subject to the greatest danger. Since he
30 has now deflected such a powerful blow and has got his breath back somewhat he is ready at any time to take up the war again, whenever he chooses. For this there would certainly be no lack of pretext, if only he could find the necessary means for his disposal.[6]

Mazarin was clearly disappointed that the war was over and wanted it to continue. He suggests that by making peace now the Emperor has been saved from 'total collapse'. This was not the outcome Mazarin wanted and he complains that he has heard that the Emperor himself considered the peace to be 'advantageous'. Because of this, Mazarin continues, the Emperor could take up the war again whenever he chose (though the Cardinal recognises that Ferdinand is not in a position to do so). And who does Mazarin blame for this unsatisfactory outcome? The Swedes. Here quite clearly Mazarin is being disingenuous (i.e. untruthful). Despite the letter being a private communication and not for publication, thereby fulfilling all the usual examination criteria for reliability, it is, in this matter, quite unreliable! In blaming the Swedes – who undoubtedly did want a settlement (see page 81) – Mazarin avoids making any reference to the real reason for the hurried nature of the settlement: the collapse of governmental authority and the outbreak of civil disorder in France itself. No doubt these inconvenient facts are overlooked because Mazarin himself was to some extent to blame for them.

As far as Sweden was concerned, Queen Christina's desire for a quick settlement did undoubtedly lessen her country's chances of a satisfactory outcome, but compared with, say, Swedish aims in 1630 or the difficult times between 1634 and 1638, the outcome was highly satisfactory. Only compared with the grandiose ambitions of 1632 and the greater expectations of the later 1640s was the outcome a disappointment. And in any event, the rapid conclusion to the peace had more to do with France than Sweden, as we have suggested.

The Peace of Westphalia proved to be lasting as far as Germany was concerned, although German particularism (i.e. political division) was reinforced and foreign interference became a fact of life. However, it could do nothing to curb the ongoing ambitions of Sweden and France which were destined to disturb the peace of Europe for some time to come.

References

1 Quoted in Geoffrey Parker, *The Thirty Years' War*, p. 179.
2 *Ibid.*, p. 178.
3 *Ibid.*, p. 184.
4 Quoted in Peter Limm, *The Thirty Years' War* (Longman, 1984), p. 104.
5 Quoted in J.H. Robinson, *Readings in European History Volume Two* (Ginn & Co., 1906), pp. 214–16.
6 Quoted in Gerhard Benecke, *Germany in the Thirty Years' War* (Arnold, 1978), pp. 18–19.

Summary Diagram
The Peace of Westphalia

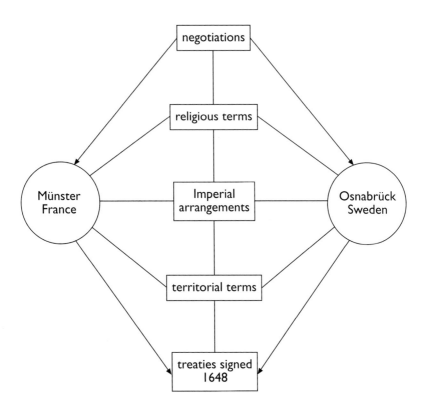

Answering essay questions on Chapter 6

1. 'It is far from clear who won the Thirty Years' War, but obvious the Habsburgs lost it.' Discuss.
2. Who gained and who lost by the Peace of Westphalia?
3. What were the consequences of the Peace of Westphalia?

This last question is not only concerned with political consequences, i.e. the terms of the treaty and their effect on the Holy Roman Empire, France, and Sweden as well as changes in international status. It is also concerned with religious, military, financial, economic and social consequences – which are the subject of the next chapter.

Source-based questions on Chapter 6

1. Peace Negotiations 1644–1648

Read the extracts from the letter from Oxenstierna on page 74, from Salvius to Queen Christina on page 80, from Christina on page 81 and from Mazarin to Servien on page 86. Answer the following questions:

a) What, according to the letter from Queen Christina, does she want her negotiatiors to do? (*4 marks*)

b) What were the 'advantageous' conditions for the Emperor in the Peace of Westphalia referred to by Mazarin in his letter (page 86, line 26)? (*6 marks*)

c) What does a comparison between the letters of Oxenstierna, Salvius and Queen Christina reveal about Swedish attitudes to the peace negotiations? (*7 marks*)

d) How fully do all the letters explain why the Peace of Westphalia took so long to conclude? (*8 marks*)

2. The Peace of Westphalia 1648

Read the extracts from the peace treaty on page 82, from Mazarin's letter on page 86 and from the Papal Bull on page 84. Answer the following questions:

a) According to the extract from the Treaty, what were the limitations imposed upon the imperial states making their own alliances? (*4 marks*)

b) What did Sweden gain when the negotiations referred to in this document were concluded? (*6 marks*)

c) How useful are the extracts from Mazarin and the Pope as evidence of their differing attitudes to the Treaty of Westphalia? (*7 marks*)

d) How fully do these extracts show the difficulties in negotiating the Peace of Westphalia? (*8 marks*)

7 The Nature of the War

POINTS TO CONSIDER

This chapter is thematic rather than a chronological narrative. It gives you the opportunity to consider the role of religion and also the military, financial, economic and social consequences of the war. What you have to decide is how far we can make any judgements about the issues raised.

1 A Religious War?

KEY ISSUE Was the Thirty Years' War a war of religion?

How far the Thirty Years' War was a war of religion is a difficult matter to determine. For one thing, in early modern times religion and politics were inextricably intertwined, so much so that our present-day approach, which makes a clear distinction between the two, is often inappropriate. Secondly, early modern language was couched in religious terminology to such an extent that it is often difficult to distinguish between what was, perhaps, formulaic or habitual and what was sincere and meaningful. And thirdly, from our secular (i.e. non-religious) age, it is quite simply very difficult to appreciate the extent and depth of religious feeling in the seventeenth century.

Was this the last religious war? Given that Protestant England and Catholic Spain had made peace in 1604, and the Protestant Dutch rebels had reached an accommodation with Catholic Spain in 1609, it could be argued that the outbreak of war in Germany, in which the fate of Protestantism seemed to be at stake, brought religious issues back to the forefront of European politics. Did the war begin as a religious war and end up a political one? At no stage was the war an exclusively religious conflict, though religion was the dominant element at times, alignments were often confessional, and many contemporaries perceived it as a confessional struggle. Historians have usually suggested that the Thirty Years' War began as a religious war, but became more secular as it progressed, and while we might decide that it was perhaps a little more complex than this, nevertheless this formulation is a useful one.

If we begin at the beginning, we can clearly see that religious issues were fundamental to the Bohemian Revolt. Religious toleration within the Habsburg lands became a major issue in the first decade of the seventeenth century (see pages 26–31) but the growth of Protestantism in Austria, Hungary and Bohemia represented a political challenge to Habsburg sovereignty as well – so that events clearly had political implications too. However, it was the Catholic reaction in Bohemia – the pulling down of Protestant churches, the election of the Jesuit-educated Ferdinand of Styria as king-designate, the appointment of a (largely) Catholic regency council and the banning of Protestants from civic office – that led to the outbreak of hostilities. Moreover, the way events unfolded was interpreted in religious terms too. In the defenestration of Prague, the fact that the Catholic regents survived the fall was clearly interpreted as divine intervention (see the extract on page 31). Similarly the defeat of the Protestants at White Mountain in 1620 was to some extent credited to the intervention of a priest:

1 When the armies of the League and the empire had united for the pur-
    pose of attacking the enemy, and the enemy had arrived before the
    walls of Prague, some of the highest officers [of the League] were
    averse to the hazard of battle. When Father Dominicus observed this,
5 he came up and humbly and modestly requested that it might be per-
    mitted him to say a few words, although he had not been called to the
    council. When permission was given him, he exhorted the leaders with
    a fiery zeal that they put their trust in God and the righteousness of
    their cause; they should firmly trust that the grace of God would not
10 be withheld, and that their hopes would be rewarded with victory.
    These words moved those who opposed the battle to yield, and with
    united forces to close upon the foe.[1]

The issue here, then, seems pretty clear: the revolt was a struggle between Catholics and Protestants. Or was it? Even at the beginning of the war when it might be viewed as being at its 'most religious' we discover that John George of Saxony, a Protestant, allied with the Catholic Emperor to defeat the Protestant rebels of Bohemia in return for some of their territory (see page 40). Clearly this was a political decision by John George. He did not like rebels, nor indeed, as a Lutheran, did he like Calvinists. So he opposed Frederick of the Palatinate whom the rebels embraced as their leader because he was a Calvinist – but not just because he was Calvinist. Quite clearly by placing himself at the head of a Protestant revolt Frederick had challenged what John George felt to be was his rightful leadership of the Protestant princes in Germany. From this example it can be appreciated that the war cannot be easily reduced to a simple formula.

Possibly the easiest way into this topic is to look at the principal participants and try to determine their motives. There is no doubting the Emperor Ferdinand II's motivation; he was devoted to the Catholic church; he was to all intents and purposes the arch-exponent of Counter Reformation Catholicism (see page 38). Quite simply, he equated Protestantism with disloyalty and he saw it as his duty to revive and reimpose the 'true faith' throughout the Empire where this was possible. Thus the success of the Spanish, Imperial and Catholic League armies in the 1620s came to be seen as victories for the Counter Reformation too, and spawned contrary Protestant align-ments. But, as we have seen, the equation of Habsburg success with the cause of Catholicism became too much even for some Catholics – particularly Maximilian of Bavaria and especially Cardinal Richelieu of France.

The Edict of Restitution in 1629 represented the peak of religios-ity in the war. But what was to Ferdinand a genuinely religious measure, a means of imposing religious uniformity, was seen by the Princes of the Empire as a way of establishing Imperial absolutism – they saw it primarily as a political measure. Thus not only were neu-tral, moderate Protestants alienated, but Catholic allies too. The opposition to the Edict came as a great disappointment to Ferdinand. Indeed when he made the Peace of Prague with Protestants in 1635, and was prepared to suspend the Edict for 40 years, it is a clear indi-cation that the nature of the war had changed. If Ferdinand was pre-pared to compromise and drop his ideals for a practical settlement, then clearly it had become a different war.

What had changed matters was the intervention of Sweden and France. From the time of his intervention, Gustavus Adolphus has been portrayed as not only the champion of Protestantism but its sav-iour too. More recently this interpretation has been called into ques-tion; it has been pointed out that Swedish security was his main motive and that his deal with Catholic France was an indication of the pragmatic nature of much of this policy. Thus, recent historiography has often dismissed the confessional element in Gustavus' interven-tion. However, as we have already stated (see page 56), religion and politics were inseparable in Sweden. Catholicism – in the form of Sigismund Vasa of Poland – represented a fundamental challenge to the legitimacy of Gustavus' throne. Indeed it was fear of a Habsburg-Polish (Catholic) invasion that prompted Swedish intervention. The defence of the Protestant faith was therefore not just a propaganda ploy to win allies; it was a matter of great importance for the survival of the Swedish monarchy. Ultimately, however, Swedish policy came to be subordinate to that of France.

There is a certain irony in the fact that it was a prince of the Catholic Church who probably did most to 'deconfessionalise' the war. Cardinal Richelieu may have justified his policy by claiming that his aim to create a general universal peace was God's will, but his anti-Habsburg position was a negation of Catholic unanimity. Richelieu appears to have been the archexponent of *raison d'état*, though it was not a term he ever used. His approach appears to be entirely secular, putting French interests before everything else. However, it would probably be more accurate to state that he put his own interests above everything else. After all, he had staked his reputation and his pos-ition as first minister on the successful outcome of an anti-Habsburg policy. Accordingly, he was prepared to make deals with Protestants in order to bring down Spain and the Emperor. It was noted before also (page 49) that in the very same year the Emperor Ferdinand II issued his Edict of Restitution, an uncompromising affirmation of Catholic faith, the Cardinal was resolving the French Wars of Religion by means of compromise and toleration. It was a symbol of what was to come, and after 1635, as French influence grew, the war took on an increasingly secular character.

Religion became important again during the peace negotiations and in the peace treaties themselves. During the negotiations a less extreme position was taken by both sides. In both Catholicism and Protestantism there seems to have been a movement away from religious persecution towards a more contemplative, inward Christianity. There was also an increasing feeling that continual warfare only barbarised the people and bankrupted governments. Accordingly, the rights of religious minorities were guaranteed – but not in a spirit of toleration, rather out of a desire to end religious confrontation and the use of religion as a political weapon. Compromise was the order of the day and machinery to reach agreement in the future was put in place. There is no doubt that after this war and, as a result of it, religious issues receded and were no longer a major destabilising influence in European politics. So, was it the last religious war? In future conflicts there would be no strong religious bond among the various allies. Of course religion continued to be politically important – for example, the fight against the Turks in the 1680s was undoubtedly a religious war with the fervour of a crusade, and William III's replacement of James II on the English throne in 1688 was certainly a matter of religion – but generally speaking the Thirty Years' War did lead to a decline in the importance of religion as an issue of war. It was certainly the last religious war in Germany. The fact that the Pope's condemnation of the peace settlement was not only ignored but anticipated and ignored in advance speaks volumes about the new religious climate. Secular issues would now come to the fore, though it should be remembered that secular questions of security, prestige, reputation and dynastic rights had also always been important even during the times of greatest religious fervour.

2 Fighting and Finance

> **KEY ISSUE** Was there a 'military revolution' in this war and how did governments find the funds to sustain so long a conflict?

a) A Military Revolution?

In a 1955 lecture Michael Roberts suggested that there had been a Military Revolution in Europe between the years 1550 and 1650, which originated with Maurice of Nassau in the Dutch Revolt and was further developed by Gustavus Adolphus during the Thirty Years' War.[2] In essence Roberts contended that Maurice had used smaller formations and greater firepower (more muskets than pikes and the use of the salvo) and that this constituted a decisive break with the past. Moreover, this approach required greater training, coordination and discipline. Gustavus Adolphus went on to develop these new methods further, but the difference between Maurice and Gustavus was more in terms of application and scale rather than innovation: Gustavus had much larger armies and fought open battles. He increased firepower with field guns, the double salvo and brigades in arrow formation. He also increased mobility and used the cavalry charge.

Geoffrey Parker to some extent endorsed this thesis, but pointed out that many of the changes Roberts referred to had in fact been developed much earlier, in the 15th century.[3] So, basically he took the starting date back to about 1450. Jeremy Black, on the other hand, has called the whole concept into question and has suggested that if there was significant change in this period, it really came later, in the second half of the seventeenth century when army sizes doubled, peacetime standing armies were developed, the bayonet replaced the pike and the soldiers got into uniform.[4]

Now this is not the place (nor is there the space) to discuss the concept of the 'Military Revolution' in any great detail, but in as far as it relates to the Thirty Years' War, it does have some relevance. Although the battle of Breitenfeld in 1631 is usually cited as the triumph of new tactics over old, what is striking about the battles of the Thirty Years' War is that the victor was usually the possessor of the larger army, regardless of tactics:

DATE	BATTLE	NUMBERS
1620	White Mountain	28,000 beat 21,000
1631	Breitenfeld	42,000 beat 35,000
1632	Lützen	9,000 on each side: a stalemate
1634	Nördlingen	33,000 beat 25,000

Despite (allegedly) being at the cutting edge of military change, the Swedes fought an inconclusive engagement in 1632 and were thoroughly defeated in 1634. When Torstennson won the battle of Jankov in 1645 with a force of 15,000, equal to that of his opponents, he did so by outmanoeuvering them and attacking from the rear. If, then, victory tended to go to the larger army, Roberts' stress on new tactics is probably misleading. It seems Jeremy Black has the better of the argument.

As far as the growth in army sizes is concerned, it is certainly true that both Wallenstein and Gustavus Adolphus were able to put together huge forces in excess of 100,000 men. However, this is mis-leading since only a small proportion would be mobile and used in battle. The rest would garrison captured territory or be involved in supply. Large areas and large numbers were needed to supply even a relatively small mobile army. Moreover, as the war progressed, army sizes actually declined, as military capacity diminished considerably. Thus army sizes reverted to about 10-15,000 men only. Moreover, what is striking about all this military activity is how indecisive battles and even whole campaigns were.

Of course, battles could be decisive – White Mountain spelt the end for the Bohemian Revolt; Breitenfeld the end for the Edict of Restitution; Nördlingen cleared the Swedes out of southern Germany; and Jankov forced the Emperor to negotiate – but gener-ally speaking battles and campaigns were inconclusive. Thus Wallenstein was unable to deliver the knock-out blow against Denmark in 1628; Nördlingen (1634) was not followed up; the Swedes' success at Wittstock in 1636 was soon reversed; their defeat of the Saxons in 1639 brought them to the gates of Prague but they were unable to capture it (or even hold Bohemia); in 1645 the French vic-tory at Allerheim could not be followed up; and after Jankov the Swedes advanced to Vienna but then had to retire. Victories then were most often not followed up at all. Why was this?

Basically the inconclusive character of warfare owed much to prob-lems with the supply of men, money and provisions, and to the strength of fortifications. Logistics (supply) and finance were the real problems. The early modern state was just inadequate to the task. Whatever military innovations there were, logistics counted for more. There could be no total victories, no total defeats. It is no wonder war-fare was indecisive, when armies were constantly in search of supplies. Indeed the war became a struggle for resources as whole regions were devastated. Defending and keeping areas for supply often took prece-dence over the development of an offensive strategy.

So far from witnessing a military revolution, what we can say about the Thirty Years' War is that it was probably one of the longest and most indecisive wars in all history! Peace really only came about when a state of exhaustion had been reached on both sides – the Emperor had no army to speak of, and France was slipping into civil war. The inability of early modern government to provide for these armies is the subject of the next section.

b) Government Finance

Basically the governments involved in the war could not afford to raise armies from their current resources. Consequently they relied on military entrepreneurs to advance the cash to recruit volunteer mercenaries from a wide variety of nationalities. The entrepreneurs did this in the belief that they would recoup their outlay and make a profit by means of defrauding the government (by receiving pay for exaggerated numbers of soldiers), by underpaying the troops (billetting – bed and board – would often compensate for inadequate wages), by forced contributions from the locality, and by pillage when on a campaign. The greatest of the military entrepreneurs were Count Mansfeld, Bernard of Saxe-Weimar and, of course, Albrecht von Wallenstein (see the profile on page 46).

Initially the Emperor Ferdinand II was able to survive and prosper because he did not have to rely on his own meagre resources. He was able to rely on Spanish and Papal subsidies as well as the contribution of Maximilian of Bavaria, perhaps the wealthiest of the German princes. Subsequently Ferdinand enjoyed the services of the most successful entrepreneur, Count Wallenstein. All commanders exacted contributions from occupied territory, but Wallenstein extended this system to friend and foe alike, and was so efficient in his methods that his dismissal in 1630 was not unrelated to the unpopularity he had engendered by these means. In later years there was a tendency towards greater government control; for instance, after 1635 exactions were replaced by regular taxation to fund the Imperial army, but this only worked intermittently and could provide for only garrison troops. Campaigns out of a given region could not be funded and whole armies could be wiped out by famine, disease and desertion, as happened to the Imperial army in 1644. Indeed Imperial effectiveness after 1635 was greatly reduced, not only because of the loss of Wallenstein and the lack of Spanish help after 1640, but because increasingly the Swedes came to occupy territory that deprived the Emperor of tax revenue. In short, when he had to rely on his own resources, the Emperor found the going tough.

The Swedes, on the other hand, had a system of conscription which gave them a relatively cheap core of reliable native troops. Obviously under Gustavus Adolphus, the army was augmented by vast numbers of mercenaries – so much so that eventually only about 10 per cent of the army was manned by Swedes, but they remained a reliable, loyal and efficient component (and were usually the officers). Swedish taxation only provided a tiny fraction of the cost of these forces and the Swedes adopted Wallenstein's methods to exact resources from occupied territory. Indeed the motto *bellum se ipsum alet* (the war must pay for itself) was very much the basis for Swedish policy. However, after the defeat at Nördlingen this policy was no longer possible and while exactions were sufficient for the conscripts in the garrisons in northern Germany, the Swedes came to rely entirely on French subsidies to provide central funds for their mobile forces. Indeed between 1638 and 1648 the French supplied the Swedes with over 3.5 million thalers for this purpose. And yet despite this, the funds were not enough, which explains why there were several mutinies, why the Swedes were unable to follow up their successes and why they insisted on an indemnity in the peace negotiations; this was essential to make up unpaid wages.

By far the wealthiest of the participants was France; however, her government was not without some serious disadvantages: it did not have American silver mines for credit purposes as the Spanish did; it could not meet costs out of occupied territory, because the French army did not really occupy any; and its tax system was illogical and inefficient. However, France was a relatively rich country with a large population (possibly as many as 20 million) and a diverse agriculture, and was, accordingly, able to finance the war by increased domestic taxation and borrowing. Indeed French taxation more than doubled between the 1620s and the 1640s, and the inadequate means of collection led Richelieu to appoint *intendants,* accountable government appointees, in order to ensure the monies reached the treasury. Thus inadvertently the Cardinal was able to extend government control. Even so, funds were inadequate and France had to muddle through by anticipating revenue (that is to say, by borrowing on the basis of future tax receipts). Moreover, all this change did not occur without resistance from the peasants, local elites and officeholders; ultimately this opposition culminated in the collapse of state finance and government authority in 1648. The civil war that ensued (the Frondes) lasted for five years and although the Cardinals' financial system survived, we have already seen how these events led directly to the end of the Thirty Years' War (see page 8). Of course, it should also be remembered that the bulk of French expenditure was not spent in Germany, but went on the war with Spain.

So, all in all, we can see that the war was often inconclusive because adequate resources were just not available to fund what could have been a decisive campaign, and that is why the war lasted so long. It was possible to maintain – by direct finance, credit, foreign subsidies, entrepreneurs and exactions – adequate funds for either small or stationary bodies of men, but not a large mobile force that would have been needed to defeat the opposition, capture fortified cities and occupy vast areas of territory for some considerable time. Consequently only mutual exhaustion could bring about an end – and that is what happened.

3 The Economic and Social Effects of the War

> **KEY ISSUE** How far can we assess the economic and social effects of the war?

Despite a wealth of local records, historians have been unable to agree on the economic, social and demographic effects of the war. In the nineteenth century the belief was that the war had created widespread death and destruction; however, this conclusion was the result of generalising about the whole of Germany from a few particular incidents and taking unreliable contemporary sources at face-value, sources such as Grimmelshausen's *The Adventures of Simplicissimus the German* which exaggerated the scale of atrocities. Town councils also often exaggerated the damage they had suffered in order to obtain tax cuts; many deserted villages were attributed to the war, when in fact they had been empty for centuries (though the war did destroy many villages); and some rulers exaggerated the effects of the war in order to enhance their achievements in post-war restoration work (e.g. the Great Elector, Frederick William, of Brandenburg). The traditional view, then, was that Germany lost about two-thirds of her population and suffered massive economic damage which set her back about a hundred years.

More recent research in the localities has demonstrated that the amount of devastation had been inflated. There was undoubtedly a decline in population, but recent estimates are in the region of 20–40 per cent, perhaps a reduction from 18 million to 12 million, rather than the two-thirds reduction of old. In many cases what appeared to be population loss was in fact really the result of migration as inhabitants abandoned villages in campaigning areas and became refugees. And of course geographically the picture was very varied. Clearly there were war zones and these areas experienced repeated devastation but other areas were wholly untouched – for instance, northwestern Germany saw very little population loss. This was also true for Austria and the Lower Rhine. On the other hand, northeastern Germany suffered considerably: Mecklenburg and Pomerania lost about 60 per cent of their pre-war population, Brandenburg about 50 per cent. Elsewhere, in the Palatinate, Alsace, and in most of Württemberg, as well as in the area between Ulm and Nördlingen, losses ranged from 50 to 70 per cent, while Bavaria (30 per cent) and Saxony (20 per cent) were not quite so badly affected.

What were the principal causes of this population loss? Death from direct military action does not seem to have been the major reason, though there were many atrocities. In the 1620s, exactions seem to have been imposed in a relatively orderly manner (when soldiers were reasonably paid they were unlikely to burn or loot); however, from the later 1630s onwards half-starved soldiers were a real threat to the civilian population; the worst period seems to have been the years 1634–40 when all the armies seem to have experienced logistical problems. Moreover, we have to distinguish between the undisciplined behaviour of individual groups of soldiers and the systematic devastation perpetrated by an entire army. The latter was rare, but did occur in Bavaria twice, in 1632 and 1646, at the hands of the Swedish army. Thus the indiscriminate slaughter of civilians and the burning of villages and towns seem to have been the exception rather than the rule. Although many villages and smaller towns were burned down, larger towns were, as a rule, usually spared as they were considered to be valuable as fortresses and sources of wealth (Magdeburg was a singular exception).

By far the most common causes of death in the conflict were war-related food shortages (brought about by requisitioning, abandoned farmland and irreplaceable livestock losses) and epidemic diseases such as typhus, influenza and dysentry (spread by both armies and refugees) which struck the vulnerable (the very young and the very old) already weakened by malnutrition. Clearly the plague was also a factor but this had little to do with the war. In addition, most marriages became infertile and families distintegrated. In many places the normal social structure broke down.

Although the verdict now is that the effects of the war have been exaggerated or were at least not as bad as thought hitherto, we should not play down the enormous suffering the population endured during this war. Many were ruined and lost everything. The statistics to some extent disguise a myriad of personal catastrophies. And there can be no adequate appreciation of the anxiety, uncertainty and fear that was generated by the war over such a long period of time. Fear of what might happen cannot be measured. It is little wonder that contemporaries believed that they had lived through a nightmare. And experiencing this nightmare must have had an impact on traditional religious beliefs – it must have tested peoples' faith – how could a charitable God have allowed it all to happen? However, the impact of the war on personal beliefs cannot be easily measured.

If historians have achieved some consensus about demographic change, that cannot be said about the economic effects of the war – those are much harder to determine. It has been suggested that there was an overall decline in economic activity which began before the war and was a part of a long-term trend, and this seems convincing – though there were exceptions such as Hamburg and Bremen which prospered. Agriculture undoubtedly suffered: in addition to the poor climate which seems to have been prevalent in the 17th century, farmland was devastated by soldiery and peasants deserted the land. Agriculture, however, could and did recover quite quickly and traditional rural society was preserved. However, what was significant was the fact that a reduced population accentuated serfdom, as peasants were increasingly tied to the land. Changes in agriculture outside Germany tended to stem from population pressures, but the Empire remained underdeveloped and her peasantry unfree. The better off managed to survive – large landowners and wealthy peasants – but small tenants and cottagers were bankrupted and their property snapped up by others. Many lords took advantage of their peasants. In many cases wealthy families were displaced by loyal ones, an occurrance that was not just confined to Bohemia. Thus there occurred a considerable redistribution of capital and wealth. But even the very rich suffered financial losses especially from exactions – in many cases the better off managed to survive, but they more often than not lost their wealth. Many nobles and mercantile families were bankrupted. Certain occupational groups did benefit – brewers and those involved in military supplies – but overall trade was disrupted and what we see is a general disruption of economic activity and a considerable growth of debt, at personal, municipal and governmental level. The fact that the money market and the credit system was thrown into disarray as well, favoured the princes who could now be arbitrary in deciding which of their debts should be repaid. The impoverishment of leading noble families and towns redounded to their benefit. Thus overall the princes were strengthened by the war – the scope of government activity was greatly increased, the level of taxation went up enormously and the church was now more strictly under government control.

Although there is evidence to suggest that many regions of central Europe appear to have experienced a rapid recovery after 1650, those who had lived through the previous 30 years had experienced a most traumatic time and had reason to give thanks when the last Swedish troops left occupied territory in the 1650s.

References

1 Part of an account of the Battle of White Mountain by Maximilian of Bavaria, told several months after the event when Father Dominicus was being considered for canonization. Quoted in Gerhard Benecke, *Germany in the Thirty Years' War* (Arnold, 1978), p. 44.
2 M. Roberts, 'The Military Revolution 1560–1660', reprinted in M. Roberts (ed.), *Essays in Swedish History* (Wiedenfeld & Nicolson, 1967).
3 Geoffrey Parker, *The Military Revolution* (CUP, 1988).
4 Jeremy Black, *A Military Revolution?* (Macmillan, 1991).

Answering essay questions on the Chapter 7

1. To what extent was the Thirty Years' War a war of religion?
2. Why were the military campaigns of the Thirty Years' War so indecisive?
3. What were the economic and social consequences of the Thirty Years' War?

8 Conclusion

POINTS TO CONSIDER

By way of conclusion it is worth looking again at the meaning and length of the war as well as the final settlement and its impact on Germany.

1 A 'Meaningless Conflict'?

KEY ISSUE What was the war all about?

Contemporaries and subsequent generations have had difficulty in understanding what the war was all about. Was it pointless, 'a meaningless conflict,' as C.V. Wedgwood famously declared in 1938?[1] Was it indeed a single war? It was clearly episodic, but it was also a single war, a single war about religious arrangements and political power within the Holy Roman Empire. It was a war principally fought out in Germany and one which involved the Austrian Habsburg Emperor throughout. However, in origin it was a war about religious and political arrangements within the Habsburgs' own territories, in particular Bohemia – it was not even an Imperial matter, let alone a Europe-wide issue. How then did the conflict escalate? The main problem would appear to have been Austrian Habsburg weakness. The Emperor called upon others – the Spanish, the Pope, the Catholic League – to assist him, so that from the very beginning the conflict had the potential to exacerbate existing tensions elsewhere. The rebels too called on outside assistance but with markedly less success, though Frederick of the Palatinate's acceptance of the royal throne of Bohemia had really been the first major step that ensured the revolt would not remain solely a matter of internal concern to the Austrian Habsburg dynasty. However, the rebels' inability to generate much outside help does explain the emperor's almost complete success in this first phase. Indeed the war should really have been over at that point.

Why then did the war last so long? Basically because the Habsburgs were too successful for their own good – too successful in defeating the Bohemian rebels, too successful in defeating Christian IV of Denmark and too successful in inflicting near total defeat on the Swedes in 1634. The Bohemian defeat was followed by one of the most dramatic political and social reconstructions in the entire early modern period and clearly this, together with the complete defeat of the elector Palatine, represented a sharp shift in the balance of power both in religious as well as political terms. After each Habsburg success there was always an opponent willing to intervene to try to check

Habsburg power, reverse the family's success and curb Counter Reformation Catholicism – be it the Protestant Dutch, the Protestant Danes or the Protestant Swedes. Ultimately (Catholic) French resources were able to do just such a thing. Indeed peace was deferred in 1635 almost entirely because of the intervention of France – peace would now not come until France agreed to it. Thus German suffering was prolonged because of decisions made in Paris. And although we have played down the extent of the devastation and hardship created by the war, perception is often more powerful than reality and the perception was that the war had created human misery on a scale that would not soon be forgotten.

What was it about the Habsburgs that generated such fear and opposition? Ever since the time of Charles V in the sixteenth century there had developed a genuine fear of a Habsburg universal monarchy – a fear that was felt both within the Empire and without (in Paris particularly – and in Rome during the pontificate of Urban VIII, 1623–44); but whether the Habsburgs did aspire to world domination is rather unlikely – and rather impractical. For the most part the Emperors were reacting to events – to the Bohemian revolt, to Danish, Swedish and French intervention. Basically both the Spanish and Austrian branches of the family had too many of their own responsibilities and too few resources to contemplate such grandiose aspirations. However, as we have just indicated, the international nature of the Habsburg family did mean that what began as an internal dispute within the hereditary territories, very soon took on Europe-wide implications and developed into a much broader war.

Was it then part of a wider European conflict? Not really, it was essentially a German war, a war about the Holy Roman Empire. However, for Richelieu and Mazarin it *was* part of a much broader conflict – it was part of their anti-Habsburg foreign policy which ultimately represented a struggle for European hegemony with Spain. The Cardinals made the German war part of their wider struggle, but in respect of Germany, France was unsuccessful. Although the Emperor was checked, he was not displaced and the French were forced to withdraw from this conflict, thereby ending it.

2 A Lasting Peace?

KEY ISSUE Why did the peace prove to be lasting?

Was the position in Germany in 1648 so very different from that of 1618? Yes and no is probably the correct answer, but yes in the sense that the tensions created by the Reformation had been defused. The Peace of Westphalia created a loose framework for religious and political coexistence in Germany which stood the test of time remarkably well. Rather than asking why the war lasted so long, perhaps we should ask why the diplomats were so successful in reaching a lasting agreement. The Peace of Westphalia was in many ways innovatory. It was the first pan-European peace congress and there was a genuine attempt to resolve a multitude of different disputes in the hope that there would be a general settlement and lasting peace. Indeed the negotiations were lengthy and complex and had to be conducted by professionals and experts – in short, by full-time diplomats. But at the same time the peace was also very much an old-fashioned dynastic settlement – for the Hasbsburgs what was important was the possession of Bohemia; for Maximilian it was the electoral title; for the restored elector Palatine the creation of his electoral title; for Brandenburg and Sweden the issue was Pomerania. It is in terms of dynastic territorial gain that the poverty of France's achievement can be most clearly appreciated.

As we have indicated, the Emperor Ferdinand III had salvaged his father's earlier gains and the emperor was in fact in a much stronger position in the hereditary territories in 1648 than he had been in 1618. There was clearly a change here. However, the war had not wrought much change in terms of the Holy Roman Empire beyond making permanent the political compromise just about reached in 1555. The workings of the Empire were now more clearly defined (or became more cumbersome depending upon your point of view) but in terms of princely power what had been for many years *de facto* (a matter of fact) was now simply acknowledged to be *de iure* (a matter of law). 1648 was certainly different from 1629 or 1635 when Imperial power was in the ascendant, but not much different from 1618.

Sweden was now more secure, though it could be argued that she had simply extended her responsibilities and given herself more problems. As we have stated, French policy must count as a failure, though the Emperor was checked and his position less strong than in 1629 or even 1635. Still, the Empire remained and, as we have observed, the Emperor got off quite lightly. France had really achieved very little in Germany. The real achievement of the Cardinals was to bankrupt Spain. While the Peace of the Pyrenees in 1659 was still very much a peace of equals (and Spain's losses were small), the way was now open for Louis XIV to assert French hegemony. When he marched his armies into the Spanish Netherlands in 1667, it was obvious for all to see who was now top dog.

The failure of many Habsburg objectives during the war, together with the (allegedly) improved position of the princes following the Westphalian settlement, used to be taken as evidence for the general decline in Imperial power and as an explanation for the Emperor's apparent concentration on purely dynastic interests. However, scholars are beginning to call this stereotype into question, though this debate is in its infancy. The Empire not only survived but revived during the long reign of Leopold I (1658–1705). The campaigns against the Turks and France between 1685 and 1714 saw considerable Imperial cooperation and went some way towards challenging French hegemony. The Holy Roman Empire was far from moribund after 1648.

3 A Divided Germany

KEY ISSUE Did the war perpetuate German divisions?

After 1648 the territorial rulers of Germany were able to benefit from the fact that the level of taxation had been raised so dramatically during the war. However, their main fear was a resumption of the fighting. Consequently many created peacetime standing armies. This was an option available only to the larger states (principally Austria and Brandenburg, Bavaria and Saxony), though Brunswick-Lüneburg (Hanover), Hesse-Cassel, Trier, Mainz, Cologne, Salzburg and Münster all had respectable forces. Others looked to the Emperor for protection. Indeed, as we have stated, the Holy Roman Empire was very much alive and well after 1648, and continued in existence until abolished by Napoleon in 1804.

After 1648, Germany was further away than ever from economic and political unity (if that was a desirable outcome). Capital was diverted into reconstruction and to some extent Germany became an economic colony of western Europe, exporting raw materials and importing finished goods which had once been manufactured domestically. Politically divisions were perpetuated and religiously Germany was divided into a Protestant north and a Catholic south. In the process Protestantism had survived and the Counter Reformation had been checked. The Reformation could not be reversed.

Germany may have remained divided for over 200 years after Westphalia, but who is to say that devolved authority and a loose peaceful federal structure is somehow inferior to the unified nation state? Is what came after 1871 in Germany to be preferred? Clearly whether or not the Thirty Years' War retarded German development is itself a moot point.

Reference

1   C.V. Wedgewood, *The Thirty Years' War* (Cape, 1938), p. 526.

Further Reading

General

Richard Bonney, *The European Dynastic States 1494–1660* (Oxford University Press, 1990)

This book is useful in order to obtain an understanding of the background to the conflict.

Thomas Munck, *Seventeenth Century Europe* (Macmillan, 1990)

This book is specifically for the seventeenth century.

Joseph Bergin (ed.), *The Seventeenth Century* (Oxford University Press, 2001)

This recent series of essays is also focussed on the same period (as the title explicitly states).

Still useful are:

Cambridge Modern History Vol IV (1906)

The New Cambridge Modern History Vol IV (1970)

The War

There are a myriad of books on the Thirty Years' War, all with that title (and this one is no exception); the following two represent the best of that group:

Ronald G. Asch, *The Thirty Years' War: The Holy Roman Empire and Europe, 1618–48* (Macmillan, 1997)

This is a recent, up-to-date survey of manageable length which keeps the focus on Germany.

Geoffrey Parker (ed.), *The Thirty Years' War* (Routledge, 1984 and 1997)

This is a full, detailed account with a number of specialist contributions. Both Asch and Parker have full bibliographies.

Gerhard Benecke, *Germany in the Thirty Years' War* (Edward Arnold, 1978)

This book is really all that is available in the English language for source material, though Parker does cite numerous extracts.

For the Military Revolution, see:

Jeremy Black, *A Military Revolution?* (Macmillan, 1991)

Biography

Michael Roberts, *Gustavus Adolphus* (Longman, 1992)

R.J. Knecht, *Richelieu* (Longman, 1991)

These are two very useful biographies in the *Profiles in Power* series.

Golo Mann, *Wallenstein* (Deutsch, 1976)

This book is probably rather too long at over 900 pages.

Geoffrey Treasure, *Mazarin* (Routledge, 1995)

This book is rather unsatisfactory on Mazarin's role in the Peace of Westphalia.

Individual Countries

Michael Hughes, *Early Modern Germany, 1477–1806* (Macmillan, 1992)

John Gagliardo, *Germany Under the Old Regime* (Longman, 1991)

Both these books on Germany are useful.

On the Holy Roman Empire, the following book is a brief, but first-class survey of recent scholarship on the subject:

Peter H. Wilson, *The Holy Roman Empire, 1495–1806* (Macmillan, 1999)

For Austria, see:

R.J.W. Evans, *The Making of the Habsburg Monarchy 1550–1700* (Clarendon Press, 1979)

Robert Bireley, *Religion and Politics in the Age of the Counter Reformation: Emperor Ferdinand II, William Lamormaini, S.J., and the Formation of Imperial Policy* (University of North Carolina Press, 1981)

For France, see:

Yves-Marie Bercé, *The Birth of Absolutism: A History of France, 1598–1661* (Macmillan, 1996)

For Spain, see:

Graham Darby, *Spain in the Seventeenth Century* (Longman, 1994)

For the Dutch, see:

Jonathan Israel, *The Dutch Republic and the Hispanic World* (Clarendon Press, 1982)

Glossary

Absolutism a term used by historians to refer to growth in centralised monarchical power at the expense of privileged groups and the periphery; it was a tendency rather than an actuality and it would be wrong to suggest that historians agree either on its meaning or indeed its existence!

Calvinism the Christian doctrines of John Calvin (1509–64), the French Protestant reformer, whose belief in predestination maintained that the chosen few were already elected to go to heaven, whereas the rest were destined for eternal damnation.

Catholicism the Christian doctrines of the Church of Rome with its emphasis on ritual, good works and confession. The head of the Church is the Pope.

Counter Reformation the name given to the process of Catholic renewal and fight-back against Protestantism.

dévot name given to the extreme Catholic faction at the French court opposed to toleration for the Huguenots and the anti-Habsburg foreign policy.

erbländer the name given to the Austrian Habsburgs' hereditary territories, sometimes rendered as *erblande*. Prior to the war this did not include Bohemia and its dependencies as this was an elective monarchy. However, in the book the term 'hereditary territories' has been used rather loosely and has occasionally included Bohemia though this is technically incorrect.

Fronde(s) the name given to the French Civil War of 1648–53, so-called after the catapults or slings used by Parisian children during the unrest.

Jesuits a Jesuit is a member of the Society of Jesus, a Roman Catholic Order of religious men founded in the 1530s. The Society was in the forefront of the Catholic fight-back against Protestantism.

Kreise areas of territory in the Holy Roman Empire organised into Circles for defensive reasons (see page 11).

Lutheranism the Protestant doctrines of Martin Luther (1483–1546) whose opposition to the Catholic Church initiated the Reformation.

Protestantism the name given to those Christians who protested against the Roman Catholic Church, severed their connection with it, and adhered to the reformed doctrines of the Reformation.

raison d'état literally 'reason of state', policies undertaken for the sake of the state, rather than for any general religious or political principles.

Reformation the movement begun in 1517 by Martin Luther, who wished to reform the Roman Catholic Church – but ultimately established his own. It became a great Europe-wide religious movement and spawned a variety of Protestant churches.

Reichshofrat Supreme Court of the Holy Roman Empire (see page 11).

Reichskammergericht as above (also see page 11).

Reichstag the representative (but not democratic) body of the Holy

Roman Empire, i.e. its parliament. Sometimes referred to as the Imperial Diet, the latter word from the Latin, *dies*, meaning a day, referring to the fact that sessions either lasted a day or the body met on a certain day (see page 10).

Uzkok War Uzkoks were Serb refugees who, as vassals of Archduke Ferdinand, attacked Turkish shipping. Unfortunately they also attacked Venetian shipping and this led to a Venetian declaration of war in 1615. This is the background to the Oñate Treaty of 1617; Ferdinand needed Spanish help to persuade the Venetians to reach a settlement (1618).

A Note on Currency
There were approximately 5 thalers to the £, and 12 livres to the £. Hence a thaler was about 2½ livres. Thus the Treaty of Bärwalde promised the Swedes just under £100,000 per annum; the Swedes themselves wanted an indemnity at the end of the war in the amount of £6 million, but settled for £1 million.

Index